DUBLIN

in your pocket

MICHELIN

Travel Publications

MAIN CONTRIBUTOR: PAUL MURPHY

PHOTOGRAPH CREDITS
Photos supplied by The Travel Library:
12, 23, 74, 82, 83, 85, 91, 124; Sean Allen 17, 39; Stuart
Black front cover; Philip Enticknap 27; Luke Kelly 30,
31, 33, 34(b), 46, 57, 84, 92, 98, 104, 110; Vincent
MacNamara 41, 52, 64, 76, 80, 86, 119; Erik Schaffer 96,
David Toase back cover, 7, 20, 25, 32, 34(t), 35, 36, 38,
40, 44, 45, 48, 49, 50, 51, 53, 54, 55, 58, 60, 66, 67, 68, 71,
72, 73, 77(t,b), 78, 79, 94, 97, 107, 113, 121; Ian Yates
title page, 43, 63.
Other Photos:
Bridgeman Art Library, London/New York 11, 14, 28,
62; Paul Murphy 5, 8, 16, 18, 19, 61, 88, 101, 103.

*Front cover: The Temple Bar pub; back cover: Trinity College;
title page: Anna Livia Fountain.*

MANUFACTURE FRANÇAISE DES PNEUMATIQUES MICHELIN

Place des Carmes-Déchaux – 63000 Clermont-Ferrand (France)

© Michelin et Cie. Propriétaires-Éditeurs 2000

Dépôt légal Jan 2000 – ISBN 2-06-653101-4 – ISSN 1272-1689

No part of this publication may be reproduced in any form

without the prior permission of the publisher.

Printed in Spain 01-00

MICHELIN TYRE PLC
Travel Publications
The Edward Hyde Building
38 Clarendon Road
WATFORD Herts WD1 1SX - UK
☎ (01923) 415000

MICHELIN TRAVEL PUBLICATIONS
Editorial Department
One Parkway South
GREENVILLE, SC 29615
☎ 1-800 423-0485

CONTENTS

Introduction *4*

BACKGROUND
Geography *6*
History *6*
The Easter Rising 16
People and Culture *20*
City Music 22

EXPLORING DUBLIN
Must See *24*
Georgian Dublin *26*
Old Town *42*
Temple Bar *51*
North Bank *54*
City of Ink 62
West of the City Centre
  South of the River *64*
  North of the River *68*
In and Around Dublin Bay
  Howth *74*
  Malahide *75*
  Marino Casino *76*
  Dún Laoghaire *77*
  Sandycove *78*
  Dalkey *78*

Excursions from Dublin
  Wicklow Mountains *80*
  Glendalough *82*
  Powerscourt *84*
  Russborough House *86*
  Newgrange *87*
  Castletown House *89*

ENJOYING YOUR VISIT
The Spirit of Dublin *90*
Weather *91*
Calendar of Events *92*
Accommodation *93*
Food and Drink *95*
Entertainment and Nightlife *102*
Children *106*
Shopping *106*
Sport *109*

A-Z FACTFINDER
The Basics *112*
A-Z Information *114*

Index *127*

INTRODUCTION

Writing in the early part of this century, James Joyce called his native town 'dear dirty Dublin'. As we approach another new century, what on earth would he have made of this new booming city, at the forefront of one of the fastest growing economies in the industrialised world, recently voted Europe's hippest city by several fashion magazines and finally, 150 years after the Great Famine, attracting back its lost children? Joyce had to leave Dublin to make his name. Today's Irish high-flyers can stay at home.

Dublin is a confident city; you can feel it in the broad elegant Georgian streets (there are more here than in either Edinburgh or Bath); in the crowded city centre pavements and bridges where the bustle of daily workers and Saturday shoppers reaches alarming proportions; and in the city centre pubs which have to close their doors every few minutes on Friday and Saturday nights because not one more reveller can be squeezed in. On Grafton Street, Bewley's Café is claimed to be the busiest in the world, and in the tourism sector, where there was once unemployment, there is now a shortage of labour. It seems only a matter of time before travellers will arrive at Dublin airport to find signs saying 'City full, please come back later'.

Fortunately, peace can also be found without too much trouble in the very heart of town. St Stephen's Green, Merrion Square and Trinity College are all oases of tranquillity. Do try, though, to explore outside the city, if you have time. The pace of life slows immediately and, particularly in the Wicklow Mountains, there are acres of

The graceful Ha'penny Bridge takes pedestrians over the Liffey.

the famed Emerald Isle scenery.

Finally, don't forget that while you may visit Paris or London to see the sights, you visit Dublin to feel the spirit of the place. You can leave Dublin content without seeing the Book of Kells, you can happily ignore the National Gallery, you can even miss the Ha'penny Bridge, but if you leave it without a laugh and a joke in the pub, or attending a traditional music session, then you really haven't experienced the craic at all.

GEOGRAPHY

Dublin lies on the east coast of the Republic of Ireland, formerly Eire (pronounced *air-er*) and also known as Southern Ireland. The city faces the Irish Sea, which divides it from Wales and the rest of Britain. Holyhead is the nearest point on the British mainland, some 96km (60 miles) due east.

Looking along the River Liffey at night, from Arran Quay.

The city is protected from the Irish Sea by Dublin Bay, a 10km- (6 mile) long bite out of the eastern coastline, and the city centre is set a mile or so back from the shore, straddling the River Liffey. To the north the Royal Canal and to the south the Grand Canal form almost a three-quarter circle (the north-west quadrant is incomplete) which marks the approximate boundary of the city centre.

Dublin is compact and relatively small, covering some 114 sq km (44 sq miles), and is as flat as a potato pancake, though its southern backdrop is hilly, with the clearly visible peaks of the Wicklow Mountains often capped with snow in winter. To the north, in County Meath, are the rolling hills and rich pasture lands of the Emerald Isle, to the west are the plains and bogs of County Kildare.

HISTORY

Celts and Christians

The **Celtic** tribes, or **Gaels**, are thought to have arrived in Ireland from Europe around 350 BC, and established two settlements in the area now known as Dublin. The one which gave the city its modern name was on the site of the present castle, by a black pool (the *Dubh Linn*) formed by the River Poddle.

The name of the other settlement, Baile Atha Cliath, meaning 'the ford of the hurdles', lives on today and may be spotted on municipal buildings and public transport vehicles.

In 55 BC the **Romans** invaded Britain and named Ireland Hibernia. They traded with Hibernia but whether or not they chose not

to invade the country is uncertain.
Christianity reached the island with
St Patrick in AD 432, and by tradition
St Patrick's Cathedral is one of the places
where the saint baptised the Irish heathens.
The next 500 years saw the great monastic
age, with monasteries such as Glendalough
attracting followers and students from all
over Europe.

Celtic crosses at Glendalough, one of Ireland's most important and mystical historic sites.

The Vikings

It is generally held that the first important
settlement in the modern-day Dublin area
was by **Vikings** from Norway who, around
841, built the first *longphort*, or harbour.
They intended to use it as a base to conquer
the rest of Ireland but this ambition was
never realised. The Vikings were driven out
early in the 10C but returned around 917
and began their largest phase of building in

Feel the soothing spirit of a thousand years of Christianity among the ancient stones of Glendalough.

the Dubh Linn area. The Norsemen began to integrate with the local Gael peoples, though nonetheless continued their raids until their defeat at the Battle of Clontarf, in 1014, by the legendary Celtic king, Brian Ború.

The Normans and the Middle Ages

In 1168 **Dermot MacMurrough**, High King of Leinster (the ancient Gael kingdom in which Dublin lies) fled to the court of Henry II of England whom he invited to help him fight his enemies. Henry's lieutenant, **Richard Fitzgilbert de Clare** ('Strongbow') conquered Dublin in 1170 and, on the death of MacMurrough, he inherited the city. The rest of the kingdom proved more difficult to take, however, and the small part beyond the city under Anglo-Norman rule later became known as the Pale, so introducing the term 'beyond the pale' meaning outside the bounds of acceptable behaviour.

Over the following centuries of the Middle Ages the city itself was only just under control, being an overcrowded, brutal place of great poverty. The 14C was particularly harsh, with terrible **famines**, followed by the Black Death, which alone killed one in three of the Irish and Dublin population.

Relations between the Irish and the English, always strained, plumbed new depths in 1366 with the **Statute of Kilkenny** which prohibited most things Irish, including the language and costume.

The Tudors and Stuarts

By the time **Henry VIII** came to power in 1509 Dublin was fast expanding. But

Henry's Reformation of the Church brought a new religious perspective to the Anglo-Irish enmity, and in 1541, for the first time, an English monarch declared himself King of Ireland (until then the title, conferred by the Pope in 1159, had been Lord of Ireland). Furthermore, Henry coerced the Irish lords to submit to the crown and then regranted their lands to them on their promise of obedience.

There were many rebellions against Henry's attempts to 'anglicise' the Irish and it was under his daughter **Elizabeth I** that the conquest was completed. Initially she tried to proceed by negotiation and by plantation, whereby land confiscated from rebellious landholders was granted to settlers, known as planters. Ulster, however, resisted and there her tactics were harsh; in the course of four wars many atrocities were committed against the natives. The conclusive English victory came in 1601 at the **Battle of Kinsale**. Dublin at this time was an important garrison and, with its large English merchant population and Elizabeth's attempt to stamp out all things Irish, the city took on an English flavour.

Under James I, Protestant Scottish and English settlers were given land in the northern counties of Ireland. In 1641, a backlash by the dispossessed natives resulted in the murder of many planters. In retaliation, **Oliver Cromwell** descended on the island in 1649 with a force of 20 000 and slaughtered many men, women and children, most notably in Drogheda and Wexford. Survivors were sent into slavery in the English colonies or banished to the west of Ireland. Even today, the name Cromwell is among the most hated in Ireland.

The triumphant King William III (1650-1702) at the Battle of the Boyne, 1 July 1690.

A ray of hope shone for the beleaguered Irish Catholic population when in 1685 James II, a Roman Catholic, acceded to the throne in England. But these were dashed once more at the famous **Battle of the Boyne** in 1690, when the Catholic forces of James II were defeated by the Protestant king, William III ('King Billy'), from the Dutch House of Orange. The result of this battle reverberates even today in Ireland and is noisily celebrated by Protestant Orangemen during the controversial and volatile 'marching season'.

Harsh new restrictions, known as the **Penal Laws**, were introduced forbidding Catholics to practise their faith. They were also disqualified from buying land and, once again, all things Gaelic were proscribed. The Protestant dominance of Ireland continued into the 19C.

Georgian Times

With the rebellious Irish firmly subdued and the horrors of the 17C passed, Dublin began to prosper from the great investments of the Anglo-Irish community as the **Golden Age** of Dublin dawned. Terraces of fine Georgian houses sprang up; parks and residential garden squares, such as St Stephen's Green, Parnell Square and Merrion Square were laid out; great public buildings, such as the

Fine Georgian doorways, such as this one on Fitzwilliam Square, are a reminder of the city's Golden Age.

Custom House and the Four Courts, were erected. The arts were extensively patronised and architecture, fine art, literature and music (of the non-Celtic kind) all flourished. Even healthcare standards reached new heights; the Rotunda Hospital became the first purpose-built maternity hospital in Europe.

In 1782 Ireland achieved an independent parliament, led by **Henry Grattan**. Although its bills could still be vetoed by the parliament in England, it introduced modest measures to help the downtrodden Catholic society, but before any real progress could be made the French Revolution of 1789 sent shock waves around Europe.

Fearing a similar revolution in its own backyard, England was unwilling to accept reform in Ireland. Many of the Protestant Anglo-Irish elite (known as 'The Ascendancy') crossed back over the Irish Sea to England. Dublin's Golden Age was over.

Rebellion and Famine

Throughout the century the seeds of rebellion and discontent had been growing. In 1791 the **United Irishmen** movement was formed in Belfast by Theobald Wolfe Tone, a Protestant barrister from Dublin. In 1798 they took up arms against the English but were defeated, with the loss of some 30 000 lives, including Tone. Reforms won by the former parliament were revoked, and under the 1800 **Act of Union** direct rule was imposed by England. In 1803 another abortive rebellion was led by **Robert Emmet**, who was hanged, but not before delivering a speech which was an inspiration for all future nationalists (and which is engraved on his statue in O'Connell Street).

Meanwhile, Daniel O'Connell (1775-1847) campaigned for the Catholic cause and the repeal of the Act of Union by peaceful means; he became the first Catholic MP (Member of Parliament) in modern times and was also the first Catholic mayor of Dublin.

In mid century, however, even political matters were overshadowed by the **Great Famine**. The Irish reliance for sustenance on a single crop made the population vulnerable when, between 1845 and 1849, potato blight destroyed the vast majority of their staple food. Between 800 000 and 1.5 million died of hunger and disease, and another 1 to 1.5 million fled to England, Canada and the USA.

The reluctance of the British government to give food or assistance quite naturally led to bitterness and anger. The call for Irish

The Irish Famine, depicted by George Frederick Watts (1817-1904).

Home Rule gathered apace and was championed by the MP **Charles Stewart Parnell** (1846-91). However, just as a breakthrough seemed imminent, Parnell was embroiled in personal scandal and lost his support in Westminster. The chance was gone but Parnell's campaigns were not totally in vain, for by now many British politicians were also in favour of Home Rule.

The Road to Independence

In 1905-08 the **Sinn Fein** movement (pronounced *shin-fayn*, meaning 'ourselves') was founded by Arthur Griffith to continue pressing Ireland's claims for independence. Success again seemed imminent when the British Parliament approved the Third Home Rule in 1914 but it was suspended owing to the outbreak of the First World War. In militant quarters Irish patience was growing thin and the stage was set for the 1916 **Easter Rising** (*see* p.16).

From the ashes of the Easter Rising the desire for independence grew ever stronger, and in 1917 **Eamon de Valera**, **Michael Collins** and others who had taken part in the rebellion were set free as part of a general amnesty. In the general election of 1918, under the Sinn Fein banner, they won 75 per cent of the national vote. Spurning the opportunity to take their seats in the British parliament, however, they formed the first Irish Assembly and in 1919 once more made a **Declaration of Independence**. With the First World War over, but still no signs of the British granting independence, the military wing of Sinn Fein (later to become the Irish Republic Army), led by Michael Collins, decided to press their claims with violence.

The Easter Rising

The Easter Rising of 1916 was a significant event in modern Irish history and was led by three groups: the Irish Republican Brotherhood (IRB), the Irish Citizens Army and the Irish Volunteers. Its principal leaders were Patrick (Padraig) Pearse, Joseph Plunkett and James Connolly. The Volunteers had by far the largest number of men at their disposal (some 10 000), but its commander Eoin MacNeill was reluctant to join arms.

Things began badly when a cargo of arms from Germany (with whom the United Kingdom was at war) was captured. Then at the last minute MacNeill attempted to pull his men out by placing an advertisement in the Sunday newspaper, cancelling his force's 'Easter exercises'. As a result, only a small minority of them turned up the next day, Easter Monday, so the uprising was confined to Dublin.

In all the rebels numbered around 1 720 men. They occupied a number of buildings in the city centre, including the Four Courts and Jameson's Distillery, and made their headquarters in the General Post Office in O'Connell Street. From here, Pearse famously read out the Declaration of Independence for the new Republic.

The British response was to dispatch an army of 20 000 troops. The battle was no contest, although the GPO did hold out for six days until heavy artillery was brought in

Eamon de Valera under arrest at Richmond Barracks.

and the interior caught fire. By the end of the week some 60-65 rebels, 130 British soldiers and 300 civilians had been killed, with a further 2 600 wounded on all sides. Many of the buildings in central Dublin were badly damaged and public opinion, at best lukewarm before the fighting, now actually turned against the rebels. The 15 ringleaders, including Pearse, Connolly, Plunkett and Eamon de Valera, were all sentenced to death. Only the American-born de Valera survived, pardoned as a result of his dual nationality.

However, the executions proved to be a major political blunder and, as Patrick Pearse had hoped all along, had the effect of swinging public sympathy almost

full circle. Kilmainham Gaol, where the ringleaders were detained and executed, once again became a place of martyrdom, support for the Republican cause redoubled and the political mood was set for the subsequent War of Independence.

The National flag flies above the General Post Office in O'Connell Street.

Policemen and British informers were warned by the rebels that, if they continued to work for the British, they would be shot. At dawn, on 21 November 1920, 14 British officers were executed in their beds. The British response was to bring in a new anti-IRA militia, nicknamed the **Black and Tans** (after their uniform). In the most infamous incident, during a Gaelic football match at Dublin's Croke Park, they opened fire indiscriminately, killing 12 people. The **War of Independence**, as it became known, rumbled on for two years until July 1921 when, after 700 deaths on the Irish side (around half IRA, half civilians) and over 500 British police and soldiers killed, the two sides agreed to a truce.

The terms of this Anglo-Irish truce treaty gave independence only to the 26 counties of the South, calling it the Free State. The six Protestant-dominated counties of the north refused to join, opting instead to remain part of the United Kingdom. This issue caused an irreconcilable split in the Republican hierarchy. The anti-treaty faction, led by Eamon de Valera, believed

The Free State troops in action during the Irish Civil War.

The revolutionary leader, Michael Collins, was killed in an ambush in 1922.

that the victory was incomplete without independence for all Ireland. The pro-treaty Free State faction, led by Michael Collins, believed they had achieved as much as they could. Collins, as the Republican's delegate, signed the treaty, remarking 'I have signed my own death warrant.'

Once again Dublin was a battleground as an **Irish Civil War** broke out, with former Republican brothers-in-arms now killing each other. The occupation and shelling of the Four Courts, in particular, was an eerie echo of the occupation of the GPO Building in Easter 1916 (*see* p.16). The war ended in May 1923, with the Free State army prevailing but losing their leader, Michael Collins, who was assassinated in Cork in 1922.

Despite losing the war, de Valera, the consummate Irish politician, went on to win the peace. He became prime minister in 1932, and during the Second World War steered the country on a neutral path. He served as prime minister on two more occasions and was president from 1959 until 1973.

Dublin Today

By contrast with the continuing political problems in Northern Ireland, the spectre of civil unrest has long since departed from the Republic of Ireland and the economy is now booming.

One of the reasons for the current prosperity is EU-assisted funding for many capital projects. However this is only a small part of the story. Having invested heavily in tertiary education, Dublin and the Republic now has a skilled and well-educated young workforce which is reaping the benefits of major inward investment made by a whole host of American and Far Eastern new technologies corporations. Ireland is now the second largest exporter of computer software in the world, after the USA, and Dublin is leading this advance, which is not just in specialist fields. In fact, the Republic is now the fastest growing economy in Europe and has been dubbed the Celtic Tiger. The future for Dublin has never looked better.

PEOPLE AND CULTURE

Modern Dublin may be one of Europe's most fashionable capitals but you'll still find the famously friendly Irishman, and Irishwoman, alive and well in the city. It may be a cliché, but the Irish really are an open and welcoming people, more so than either the English or their Gaelic cousins elsewhere.

   Given the current Dublin demographic trend it's likely that you will meet more females than males, many more young than old people, and that the majority of these young Dubliners will be well educated. Despite all those Paddy jokes, Dubliners, by and large, are nobody's fools. Indeed, one of the cornerstones of the city's recent success is its emphasis on education. A better known Irish trait is the famously easy-going nature –

Dame Street, in the revitalised Temple Bar district.

*Spot the new
Dubliners or next
Chieftains at a
toe-tapping sing-
along Sunday
lunchtime music
session – the
perfect way to blow
away Saturday
night's cobwebs!*

'sure, and it's no problem' is a constant city refrain.

The fact that the Irish are more than just a convivial and sociable race is reflected in their love of music and dance. One of the great dance phenomena of recent years has been *Riverdance*, and even though it was led by a Chicago Irishman, Michael Flatley, it draws directly on the very finest traditions of Irish traditional 'hoofing', which you can see performed in pubs in Dublin. Music is innate in the Irish psyche and a night out in Dublin without music would be like the proverbial pub with no beer (*see* pp. 22 and 100).

Before long, you'll no doubt hear reference to what sounds like 'the crack'. It's actually spelled *craic* and is Gaelic for fun, or having a good time – as in 'let's go to Paddy Murphy's pub for the craic'. The craic is the jokes, the stories, the camaraderie, the music, the dancing and enjoying a Guinness or six. The effect of the drink may be part of the craic, but getting drunk for its own sake is definitely not. It is this subtle difference that so many English stag and hen parties have failed to comprehend and why they have outworn their welcome in the city.

Of course, life in Dublin, as in every other modern city, is imperfect; begging, usually of the peaceful and passive kind, is prevalent on the streets, and anyone averse to strong language will have to turn a deaf ear, and not just from workmen in the pubs. And take care not to abuse your hosts' easy-going nature. Given the turbulent history of this small island, conversations on politics and religion are best avoided. But on the whole, it's likely that you will leave Dublin liking its people a great deal.

City Music

Music flows through Dublin as surely as the Liffey, and is an integral feature of the city's entertainment. A typical traditional Irish folk band in a Dublin pub nowadays comprises a guitar or two, a mandolin, a banjo, a fiddle (violin), a whistle or a flute and a bodhrán (a hand-held Irish goatskin drum). You might also find included a double bass, an accordion, a harmonica (mouth organ) or, if you're lucky, the *uilleann* (elbow) pipes. Just add mellifluous voices, of which there is no shortage, and you have all the ingredients for a session which will make you laugh or cry, listen attentively or sing along and dance – perhaps all of these. The vast majority of pub players are unknown outside their own community, performing for the craic and the whip-round (collection) at the end of the session, though these days many pub bands also offer cassettes and CDs.

The best known bands are the eponymous Dubliners (now defunct) who formed in 1962 in O'Donoghue's pub,

and the Chieftains, who got together in 1964 at the Gresham Hotel and, amazingly, are still going strong today.

Dublin isn't just the home of traditional music – it also rocks in the big league. The biggest Irish band of all time are U2, who after 20 years of recording are still one of the world's top acts; to date they have sold 76 million albums.

U2 are a truly Dublin band; its members were born and raised in the city and are now resident in Killiney Bay, with business interests including the famous Clarence Hotel.

Other major Irish stars who are Dubliners, or who at least paid their musical dues in the city, include Bob Geldof (with the Boomtown Rats), Chris de Burgh (now living near Power-scourt), the late Phil Lynott of Thin Lizzy, Sinead O'Connor, Christy Moore, Mary Black, and the Cranberries.

To learn more about Dublin's musical heritage, take the Musical Pub Crawl departing from Oliver St John Gogarty's pub in Temple Bar (Sun-Fri, 7.30pm). Fans on a musical pilgrimage might also enjoy the *Rock and Stroll Trail* booklet on sale at the tourism centre. For what's happening musically in the city right now, see *Hot Press* magazine (*see* p. 103).

Buskers on Grafton Street.

MUST SEE

Trinity College★★
One of the greatest works of Celtic art, the **Book of Kells**, was described in the 11C *Irish Annals* as 'the most precious object of the western world' and is still arguably Ireland's greatest national treasure. See it and other illustrated manuscripts in the College's **Treasury★★★**, and experience the hushed, reverential atmosphere of the **Library★★★**.

Kilmainham Gaol★★
A place of shame and heroism, where some of the Republic's most famous figures were incarcerated and some of its greatest injustices were perpetrated. Brilliantly presented, no matter which side of the political divide you fall.

National Museum★★
The main museum has a fascinating collection of *Or* (Irish Gold), but it is in the new Collins Barracks annexe that the city's best displayed and most eclectic treasures are to be found.

Merrion Square★
This perfectly formed Georgian square is not just for lovers of architecture. Its 'secret gardens' are a perfect place for a sandwich or just to rest awhile after cultural overload across the road at the museums and galleries.

Ha'penny Bridge (Liffey Bridge)★

As capital city landmarks go, the Ha'penny Bridge may be slender in form, but it's big on charm. See it at dusk as the crowds hurry home, preferably from the atmospheric Winding Stair Bookshop Café.

The main gate of Trinity College, with statues of Edmund Burke (left) and Oliver Goldsmith (right).

Jameson's Literary Pub Crawl

More of a theatrical and comedy experience than a night's boozing, and the perfect way to learn about the city's rich literary heritage.

Temple Bar

Dublin's new Left Bank – whether you love it or hate it will largely depend on your mental age, how busy it is, where you end up and who you are with. See it by day for the shops and at night for its buzz.

Bewley's Cafés

If you're looking for a place with style, atmosphere, character, a touch of nostalgia *and* a nice cup of coffee, then you can't do better than Bewley's, as much a part of Dublin life as a pint of Guinness.

County Wicklow

The **Powerscourt★★** estate and the monastic remains at **Glendalough★★★** are two of Ireland's most compelling sights, each set in the glorious **Wicklow Mountains★★** countryside. Just getting there is a pleasure in itself.

Dublin Bay

Take your pick from any one (or a combination) of the charming seaside suburbs of **Dalkey**, **Malahide★★** or **Howth★**. On a sunny day, a journey aboard the DART railway is the perfect out-of-town trip.

GEORGIAN DUBLIN

Trinity College★★

Trinity College's front entrance, on College Green, is a pedestrian and traffic bottleneck, often jam-packed with people and vehicles milling to and from O'Connell Street, Grafton Street and Dame Street. Double-decker tour buses and walking tours also depart from here, adding to the general mayhem. Yet just inside its hallowed portals

The fine campanile, dating from 1853, stands in the shady grounds of Trinity College campus.

calm reigns and visitors are immersed in the city's principle centre of learning.

The handsome lawned quadrangle which you enter has all the air and architecture of an Oxford or Cambridge college – in fact it doubled for a university campus in the film *Educating Rita*. Straight ahead is the college's most striking external feature, its huge campanile, marooned in the centre of the quad.

Although Trinity College was founded in 1592 by Elizabeth I, most of the buildings date from the 18C and 19C; it remained an Anglican preserve until the late 18C. From

Portrait of St John, from the Book of Kells.

here dozens of Dublin's luminaries such as Jonathan Swift, Oliver Goldsmith, Samuel Beckett, Bram Stoker and Oscar Wilde graduated.

As far as today's visitors are concerned the main attraction is the world-famous Book of Kells, housed in the **Treasury★★★**. Resist the temptation to head straight there, however, and instead go first to **The Dublin Experience** (open summer only), an audio-visual presentation which gives an entertaining and informative whizz through a millennium of city history.

The **Book of Kells** is a magnificent lavishly-decorated illuminated manuscript of the four Gospels in Latin, on vellum (calf skin). It was produced around the early 9C by the monks of Iona who moved to Kells, County Meath, after AD 806. To minimise wear, tear and light-damage only two pages are ever on display at once and are turned approximately every two months. A fascinating and very beautiful exhibition 'Turning Darkness into Light' tells you everything you could want to know about the book, and also features four of its close relatives; the Book of Durrow, the Book of Armagh, the Book of Dimma and the Book of Mulling. Two of these four books are always on display.

The self-guided tour continues upstairs in the **Long Room★★** of **Trinity College Library★★★**. Measuring 64m by 12m (209ft by 40ft), this cavernous dark-brown galleried and barrel-vaulted chamber is a veritable temple to bibliography. Treading reverentially past its hushed floor-to-ceiling shelves, you half expect to find Jonathan Swift himself in the next alcove, but instead find his marble bust alongside Ireland's

Locals have affectionately dubbed the statue of fishmonger Molly Malone 'the tart with the cart'.

oldest harp, dating from the later Middle Ages. It was last plucked in 1961.

Bank of Ireland★★

Next to the college is the imposing Greek-style portico of the **Bank of Ireland★★**. It was built in 1728 to house the first Irish Parliament and converted to the Bank of Ireland in 1803. The House of Commons has gone, but the old **House of Lords** remains intact and the entertaining story of this building and chamber, plus much, much more, is splendidly related by the Bank's resident expert historian (Tues, 10.30am, 11.30am, 1.45pm).

In the same building is a working branch of the Bank of Ireland, set in a beautiful historic banking hall, and a permanent exhibition, **The Story of Banking**. This is an interesting if rather ponderous tour through the Bank's history (Tues-Fri, 10am-4pm), and is worth a visit if you cannot get to the Tuesday tour of the House of Lords, as it covers some of the same ground. The Bank of Ireland Arts Centre is also located on the same premises (*see* p.105).

Grafton Street★

Walk past the front of Trinity College and you will find a statue to Dublin's most celebrated street seller, sweet **Molly Malone**. The bronze is nicknamed 'the tart with the cart', for reasons that are obvious when you see the likeness, but whether or not she ever really 'wheeled her wheelbarrow through streets broad and narrow' is open to debate.

Continue straight ahead up Grafton Street, the city's principal shopping thoroughfare, stopping, whether or not you need refreshment, at **Bewley's Oriental Café**. This is the finest branch of this small city chain (*see* p.98) and opened in 1927. All of its three floors are worth exploring and it is famous for its Harry Clarke Room. Clarke was an Irish symbolist and his use of stained glass, Celtic mysticism, national romanticism, Art Nouveau and other styles

The semicircular façade of the Bank of Ireland, which was the splendid home of the Irish Parliament in the 18C.

Colourful Grafton Street is always packed with shoppers.

A grand piano entertains lunchtime diners in Powerscourt Townhouse Centre.

to furnish and decorate Bewley's makes this Dublin's most eclectic and fascinating eating establishment.

Just off Grafton Street are some of Dublin's most atmospheric and historic pubs, including McDaid's and Davey Byrne's (*see* p.100).

West of Grafton Street (signposted), on South William Street, is the **Powerscourt Townhouse Centre★**. This highly ambitious and much-acclaimed shopping complex was created from an 18C townhouse and courtyard in 1981. Go to the very top, now occupied by the Solomon Gallery, to see some fine surviving stucco ceilings, friezes

and original woodwork. Adjacent is the
Dublin Civic Museum, a small space mostly
given over to temporary exhibitions. The
only permanent exhibit of note is the head
of Nelson's Pillar which once stood on
O'Connell Street (*see* p.54).

St Stephen's Green

This great green city lung, covering 9ha
(22 acres), was laid out in 1877-80 and lined
with grand houses built in Dublin's Golden
Age. It includes a sizeable lake with wildfowl,
several statues and memorials, arboretums,
lawns, a garden for the blind, a bandstand
and a children's playground. The most

Fusilier's Arch (1907) forms a grand entrance to the popular St Stephen's Green.

A cockerel admires one of the many sculptures decorating St Stephen's Green.

famous building on the north side is the **Shelbourne Hotel**, built in 1867; uniformed doormen and exotic Nubian statues underline its pre-eminence in Dublin's accommodation league. During the 1916 Rising, British soldiers fired from the hotel's upper windows onto Republicans encamped on St Stephen's Green.

On the south side is **Newman House★★**, comprising a pair of beautifully preserved 18C town houses, famous for their spectacular Baroque and Rococo stucco

The elegant heritage of Georgian Dublin is encapsulated in Newman House.

interiors (open June-Sept). They were built in 1738 and 1765 and acquired by the Catholic University of Ireland in the mid 19C. Today they belong to University College, Dublin. The great English poet, Gerard Manley Hopkins, spent the last years of his life in residence while Professor of Classics (1884-89), and his study-cum-bedroom has been preserved for visitors. James Joyce was a student at Newman House from 1899-1902 and gave his maiden speech to the Literary and Historical Society in the handsome room known as the Physics Theatre (later used as a setting in Joyce's *Portrait of the Artist as a Young Man*).

Tucked alongside Newman House is the much overlooked **University Church**, a delightful small building designed at the behest of Cardinal Newman in Byzantine and Italian early-Christian styles.

The tree of life adorns the golden apse of the unusual Byzantine-style University Church.

Museums and Galleries

Just off St Stephen's Green, the block surrounded by Merrion Row, Upper Merrion Street/Merrion Square West, Nassau Street and Kildare Street holds four museums and galleries of national importance.

Walk down Kildare Street from St Stephen's Green, and the first of these is the **National Museum★★**, the repository of Ireland's archaeological and early historic treasures. The building itself, dating from 1890, is a museum piece, with a large open industrial-style central hall constructed of glass and iron and rather incongruously trimmed with lavish multi-coloured majolica door frames.

All that glitters in the sunken main part of the hall is gold (*Or* in Irish), a beautiful collection of shining pieces, comprising mostly *lunulae*, crescent-shaped beaten gold collars, dug out of peat bogs. It is claimed to be the finest collection of prehistoric gold artefacts in Europe. Various hoards on display also include hollow gold balls as big as oranges.

It is the **Treasury★★**, however, which is the pride of the museum and you should start with the 15-minute audio-visual introduction. Here you will find the country's most outstanding examples of Celtic and medieval craft and metalworking, with the Tara Brooch and the Ardagh Chalice (both 8C) acknowledged as the finest pieces.

The **Road to Independence** exhibition, dealing with various aspects of the struggle for independence and particularly the Easter Rising, is interesting if somewhat out of kilter with the main museum, and the topic is better covered at Kilmainham Gaol (*see* p.65).

Upstairs is devoted mostly to Viking Ireland, with the highlight being the Cross of Cong (early 12C), individually displayed to great effect. It was originally crafted to hold a fragment of the True Cross. Finally, don't miss the small but beautiful exhibition on Ancient Egypt, with several mummies on display.

Adjacent to the National Museum is the **National Library**, whose main feature is its splendid domed circular Reading Room. Only readers are admitted, but the general public are welcome to peer in and see the place where many a great Irish writer has researched and taken inspiration. Temporary exhibitions are staged and many visitors also come to the Library in search of their Irish roots, courtesy of the free genealogical service which is provided here.

Trace your Irish origins at the National Library, with its extensive archives and reference section.

Further down Kildare Street, the **State Heraldic Museum** is a colourful one-room display of various banners, crests, insignias, stamps, medals and heraldic devices.

Walk around the corner of the block, via Nassau Street, onto Merrion Square West to the **National Gallery★★**. This is a large place and unless there is a particular area that you wish to study the best bet is to head for the gallery's most important pieces as indicated on the floor plan. An alternative for getting quickly acquainted is the Multimedia

Gallery facility, where you can take a gallery overview and/or study various paintings and artists by chronology, country, theme and so on.

On the lower levels, devoted to Irish and British art, do not miss Daniel Maclise's huge and vibrant *Strongbow and Aoife*. By contrast, Gainsborough's *Cottage Girl* is an unashamed exercise in rural sentimentality. Close by are the definitive portraits of George Bernard Shaw (by John Collier) and of James Joyce (by Jacques Emile Blanche). Jack B Yeats (1871-1957), now generally considered as the most important Irish artist, is honoured in the **Yeats Museum**, a section of the gallery featuring the works of Jack and his artistic family, including his brother W B Yeats, much better known for his poetry.

The National Gallery is home to a fine collection of European art.

Most visitors flock upstairs to view the **European Old Masters** collection and its wide coverage of several European schools of painting, with some outstanding pieces by Picasso, Poussin, Vermeer, Velázquez, Titian and Rembrandt. The gallery's most famous bequest, made in 1992 (called 'the bequest of the century') is *The Taking of Christ*, by Caravaggio. There is also a good collection of Impressionist works. Every January, fans of J M W Turner descend on the gallery to view the annual exhibition of his watercolours.

Adjacent to the National Gallery is the green sweep of Leinster Lawn and the broad

Georgian frontage of **Leinster House** (pronounced *lenster*), home to the Irish Parliament or *Dáil Éireann* (pronounced *dawl erren*) it is closed to the general public.

Moving up the street the next building is the **Natural History Museum**. The stars of this thoroughly old-fashioned shrine to taxidermy are the long extinct Giant Irish Deer (don't call them elks!), whose skeletons immediately confront visitors. They had the largest antler span of any animal, living or extinct, with one Irish specimen recorded at 4.3m (14ft) across. The rest of the museum is a fascinating, densely-packed zoo of stuffed creatures of all kinds: downstairs from Ireland, upstairs from the rest of the world. It's like being inside a big-game hunter's wildest dream, or perhaps a conservationist's worst nightmare.

Adjacent are the imposing **Government Buildings**, dating from 1911. Not to be

Georgian doorways on Merrion Square.

confused with Leinster House, this complex was acquired by Parliament, from the University of Dublin, for offices in 1989. Tours are given each Saturday of the various meeting rooms, Cabinet Office and the office of the *Taoiseach* (pronounced *tee-shuck*, meaning prime minister). Pick up a ticket (free) from the National Gallery foyer.

Merrion Square★

Of Dublin's many Georgian squares, **Merrion Square★** is the finest. Laid out in 1762, delicate fanlights surmount elegant doorways and commemorative plaques mark the houses where famous Dubliners once lived: Daniel O'Connell (no 58), W B Yeats (no 82 and no 52) and Oscar Wilde, whose family lived at no 1 (Oscar was born a stone's throw away, in Westland Row). The corner of the gardens opposite no 1 is now a shrine to Wilde, with a reclining fairground-style statue of the great wit and playwright. Adjacent are two small pillars surmounted by the naked torso of a male and female respectively. Scrawled on them, what appears at first glance to be graffiti, are some of Wilde's most famous and witty epigrams.

A pensive Oscar Wilde reclines in the gardens of Merrion Square.

Merrion Square Gardens are gorgeous, laid out with large open lawns, a profusion of flowers, 'secret' glades, a children's playground and various statuary and memorials. On summer weekends, artists hang pictures for sale on the park railings.

On the south-east corner of the square, look down Upper Mount Street, and **St Stephen's Church** provides one of the city's signature vistas. Its domed tower has given it the nickname of 'the Pepper Canister'. Merrion Square is also well worth a stroll by night, when many buildings are floodlit, none to better effect than the Government Buildings.

On the corner of Merrion Square East and Lower Fitzwilliam Street is the house known simply as **Number Twenty Nine★**. This beautifully restored four-storey town house, built in 1794, now functions as a museum dedicated to domestic middle-class life in Dublin from 1790 to 1820. After an introductory audio-visual, its custodians bring the house back to life with an informative guided tour (closed Mon).

OLD TOWN

Dublin Castle★★
Dublin Castle was built around 1204, thirty years after the Anglo-Norman landing in Ireland, by order of King John, and stands at the very heart of the original city. Indeed, the name *Dubh Linn* (pronounced *dove-lin*) – from which Dublin is derived – means black pool and refers to a small dark lake which was on the site of the gardens at the back of the castle. In fact, this is the best place from which to view the castle as it is the only aspect from which you get any idea of its medieval appearance. From the main entrance, off Dame Street, it is hardly recognisable as a castle at all. This is because in 1684 much of the medieval castle was destroyed by fire, and the complex that you see today dates largely from the 18C and

Young visitors begin their tour of Dublin Castle in the Great Courtyard.

early 19C. The only notable surviving medieval part is the 13C **Record Tower** (not open to the public). Adjacent is the 19C Gothic-Revival Chapel Royal.

Until 1922, when the British handed over the keys to Michael Collins, the castle was always the symbol of British rule. In the old days, traitors' heads were put on spikes on the gates and its sinister secret atmosphere during the rebellion years following the 1916 Easter Rising was chillingly evoked in the 1996 film *Michael Collins*.

Castle tours begin in the **Great Courtyard**, which contains the principal buildings which housed the British Vice-Regal

administration. The tour comprises the State Apartments and the Powder Tower Undercroft.

The **Apartments** were built in the mid to late 18C as residential quarters and include the Drawing Room, the Throne Room, the Picture Gallery and other grandiosely decorated chambers. Today, these provide the venue for Presidential Inaugurations and State Functions.

Much older is the **Powder Tower Undercroft**, where deep excavations have uncovered part of the original Viking and

The Throne Room, one of the State Apartments on view in Dublin Castle.

Norman settlements and a 13C arch in the old city wall.

The castle has also recently become the home of the **Chester Beatty Library***, famed for its world-class collection of Islamic and Far Eastern Art. Only a small percentage of the huge collection is ever on show at any one time and exhibits are constantly changing, but you can expect to see magnificently illuminated Korans and holy books, Japanese woodblock prints, *netsuke* (carved ivory snuff boxes), Chinese rhino horn cups and a Golden Buddha.

Dublin's Viking Adventure

Towards the Liffey, on Essex Street, and set right on top of the site where the Vikings first settled in Dublin around a thousand years ago, the Viking Adventure is a humorous, entertaining and informative keyhole in time. The adventure begins aboard a longship on the high seas, amid a howling gale. You have been taken captive by a Viking and land back in his time at his settlement. Besides expressing astonishment at your strange clothes, telling you what your tasks will be in the Viking village (fetching wood, killing wolves – 'you can run fast, can't you?'), he will generally poke fun at you and then in a mock-concerned manner apologise for not asking you sooner if you wanted to use the cesspits after such a long journey! You then take a seat with his wife in their humble wattle-and-timber dwelling for

A group of friendly Vikings ready to take you back in time.

more tales of everyday Viking life. Alas, just as you are getting used to life a thousand years ago, the spell is broken and it's time to go back to the present via a more conventional exhibition which traces Dublin's timeline through a deep cross-section of the earth. Eventually, you emerge into a small museum area displaying artefacts excavated at the Wood Quay site, which was controversially covered over by the mega-complex of the Dublin Corporation offices in the early 1980s.

Christ Church Cathedral★★

Stranded by the traffic, small in comparison to the surrounding office blocks, and too neat and tidy to look any great age, the

Christ Church Cathedral's exterior belies its 12C origins.

The Tower of London

Advanced Bookings 0870 756 7070 • **Recorded Information** 0870 756 6060

Kensington Palace State Apartments

Advanced Bookings 0870 751 5180 • **Recorded Information** 0870 751 5170

Hampton Court Palace

Advanced Bookings 0870 753 7777 • **Recorded Information** 0870 752 7777

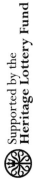

Supported by the
Heritage Lottery Fund

PLEASE RETAIN THIS TICKET. Terms and Conditions of sale – subject to English Law

1. Tickets cannot be resold, exchanged or refunded, to do so or to alter or deface the ticket will render it void.
2. In the interest of safety, the palace retains the right to refuse admission or to request visitors to leave the palace at any time.
3. Smoking, eating and drinking are prohibited within all buildings.
4. The use of photographic and recording equipment or mobile phones is prohibited within all buildings (unless otherwise advertised).
5. Commercial filming and photography is not permitted without prior agreement from the Historic Royal Palaces Press Office.
6. Historic Royal Palaces exclude all liability for any loss, damage to personal property or injury to visitors, howsoever caused, but do not exclude liability where any death or injury caused by the negligence of Historic Royal Palace, its staff or servants.

www.hrp.org.uk

VAT No. 710 9813 45

Reg Charity No. 1068852

HISTORIC ROYAL PALACES

VALID TODAY ONLY
SUNDAY 10 JUL 2005
Adult Agency

10/07/2005
ADLT AVS

10001715

Evan Evans
GIFT AID: TRANSACTION REFERENCE 83698265

:13p

Hampton Court Palace

Tower of London

Kensington Palace

HM TOWER OF LONDON ONLY

001381 TPS

2:13p

exterior of **Christ Church Cathedral★★** is something of a disappointment, given its pre-eminent status. However, an elegant Romanesque door overlooks the ruins of the Chapter House and the atmosphere of the interior is more evocative of its late 12C origins, when the church was built by Henry II's lieutenant Richard Fitzgilbert de Clare (nicknamed Strongbow, *see* p.9). Today only the south transept, the north wall and the western half of the choir remain from Strongbow's day. The rest crashed down in 1562, smashing among other things **Strongbow's monument**, and leaving only a small part of the original which lies next to the present replica monument. The cathedral's co-founder, Archbishop St Laurence O'Toole, is also here, in heart if not in body, as you will see from the coronary-shaped reliquary in the Peace Chapel behind the altar.

Below the church is the large 12C **crypt** with several curious statues, a mummified cat and rat in a chase, caught for eternity in an organ pipe in the 1860s.

The Cathedral is linked by a bridge to the Synod Hall, which now houses **Dublinia**, an exhibition relating the city's development from Strongbow's time up to the 16C. It begins with a headphone tour through a series of tableaux and concludes with hands-on medieval fayre-themed exhibits and more conventional museum pieces from the National Museum. There's also a particularly good scale-model of the early city. However, it is debatable whether the much vaunted view of the city from the top of the connected Church of St Michael's tower (which is glassed in) is worth the effort of climbing the 96 steps.

St Patrick's Cathedral★★

A short walk south along Patrick Street, turning off down St Patrick Close, **St Patrick's Cathedral★★** occupies one of the city's earliest Christian sites, dating back to the 5C, where the saint himself is supposed to have baptised converts at a well. Its site is marked in the cathedral's pleasant landscaped gardens. Like Christ Church, the cathedral was built by the Normans in the 12C and was restored by the Victorians, but it is larger (the biggest church in Ireland), grander and retains an older

Dublin's second Protestant cathedral, St Patrick's, is built on ancient hallowed ground.

atmosphere than its near neighbour.

By the entrance is the epitaph and grave of the Cathedral's famous literary dean, Jonathan Swift. Alongside is the splendid 17C **Boyle monument**, populated by over 20 painted figures.

A curiosity close by is the old Chapter House door with a hole cut in it. This was made by the Norman Earl of Kildare, in 1492, so that he could put his arm through the door as a conciliatory gesture to his enemy, Black James Ormond, who had taken refuge in the Chapter House. Not

Flags of the noble order of the Knights of St Patrick hang in the choir.

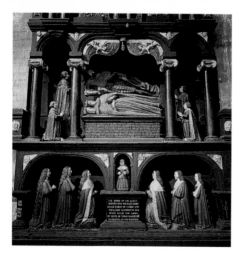

The huge Boyle monument was built by Richard Boyle, the Earl of Cork, in memory of his wife.

knowing whether his hand would be shaken or chopped off (happily, it was shaken!), it introduced the phrase 'to chance one's arm' into the English language.

Other points of interest in the cathedral include the statue of Turlough O'Carolan, 'last of the Irish bards'; the helmets, swords and banners above the choir, used until 1869 for the investiture of Knights of St Patrick; and the four 16C medieval brasses in the south choir aisle which are some of the oldest in Ireland.

Adjacent to the Cathedral is one of Dublin's hidden gems, **Marsh's Library★★** (closed Sun and Tues). It was built in 1701 to house the first public library in Ireland, taking its name from its founder, Archbishop Marsh. A total of 25 000 ancient volumes still sit on the dark oak bookcases, but the atmosphere is bright and airy and alongside the shelves of learned tomes high-

The venerable Marsh's Library houses a fine collection of antiquarian books and manuscripts.

quality exhibitions are staged. The library's most unusual feature is its 'cages' – three small cubicles where precious books can be consulted behind locked wire screens.

TEMPLE BAR

If any one area of Dublin typifies the transformation of the city into one of Europe's hippest capitals, then it is Temple Bar. Much of the area, which is bounded by the river, Dame Street, Westmoreland Street/O'Connell Bridge and Fishamble Street, was bought up in the 1960s for the creation of a giant new bus terminal. Happily that idea was scrapped, and in the 1980s Temple Bar was developed into a contemporary cultural and entertainment district devoted to pubs, nightclubs, restaurants, cafés, galleries, arts centres and small shops. Old establishments were converted or simply re-discovered, and new ones sprang up. Adjectives like 'funky', 'cutting edge' and 'state-of-the-art' became de rigeur. Like London's Covent Garden, Temple Bar has been a roaring success ever since. Recently, rock megastars U2 conferred even more street cred and panache on the area with the purchase and conversion of the Clarence Hotel into the trendiest place in the city.

Temple Bar is a small area and it's well worth wandering its narrow, cobbled, mostly pedestrianised streets by day and by night. There are many excellent small shops, plenty of the alternative/esoteric variety, great for browsing and buying, and by day you can relax in its multitude of bars and eating places (see p.100). There is an **Information Centre** at 18 Eustace Street.

Be warned, though – by night the pace becomes frenetic, the crowds build up and by 9pm at the weekend, or in high season at

Colourful Crown Alley, in the Temple Bar district – a magnet for the young.

There's no toll nowadays to stroll across the city's landmark Ha'penny Bridge.

any time, you will find it difficult even to get into the bars. In fact, for all its plus points, Temple Bar after dark has become a victim of its own success. A clampdown on revelling hen and stag parties means it is less rowdy than it was a few years ago, but nevertheless most streetwise Dubliners choose to avoid the area, particularly at weekends, leaving it to the tender care of partying tourists.

For a flavour of Temple Bar a hundred years ago, when it was a warren of small working-class shops and traders, squeeze your way through Merchant's Arch. It opens onto the river where you will come face to face with the city's most famous structure. The **Liffey Bridge★** may be its correct name, but everyone knows this charming, delicate cast-iron crossing as the **Ha'penny Bridge**. It was constructed in 1816 (originally named the Wellington Bridge) and takes its nickname after the toll of half an old penny which was levied until 1919.

NORTH BANK

O'Connell Street★

This broad bustling street has been the principal thoroughfare in Dublin since the 18C, when it was known as Sackville Street. Its quality has declined in recent years, however, and it is now disfigured by a rash of discount shops and fast-food outlets. Nonetheless, its sheer size and many monuments still give it a grand air.

At the head of the street, figuratively and literally, is the statue of **Daniel O'Connell** (1775-1847). Known as 'The Liberator', O'Connell was a brilliant orator who campaigned peacefully as the champion of Catholic rights (*see* p.14). The largest of all the street's statuary was Nelson's Pillar, an unmistakable feature of old city photographs. It was bombed several times by

Daniel O'Connell's monument stands guard on O'Connell Street, Dublin's main thoroughfare.

Republicans and was finally demolished in 1966. You can see its head in the Civic Museum (*see* p.33). Where it stood is now the **Anna Livia Fountain**, James Joyce's female personification of the Liffey, locally derided as 'the Floozy in the Jacuzzi', or the 'Whore in the Sewer' (which in the vernacular rhymes). Adjacent is another controversial modern statue, in the form of a giant polychrome bird.

In a street littered with political history, the most potent symbol of all is the **General Post Office Building★**. In the 1916 Easter Rising this became the rebels' headquarters, and its great Ionic portico still bears the scars of the six-day battle (*see* p.16). It's a fine place from which to post your cards, with paintings of the fighting and the famous bronze of *The Death of Cuchulainn* (a mythical Irish warrior) honouring the executed rebels.

The General Post Office Building still bears the scars of the 1916 Easter Rising.

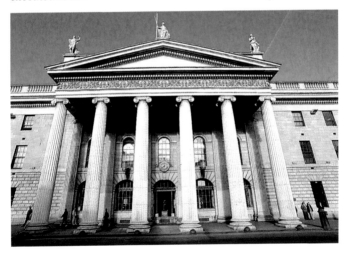

Take a short detour at this point off O'Connell Street, left to the shops and stalls of Henry Street and Moore Street. To the right, along Cathedral Street, is the city's Roman Catholic cathedral, known, somewhat confusingly, as the **Pro-Cathedral★**. It is surprisingly plain and of minor interest.

At the far end of O'Connell Street is a statue to yet another of Ireland's great political heroes, **Charles Stewart Parnell** (1846-91), the most influential Irish politician of the late 19C and leader of the Irish Nationalist Party (*see* p.15).

The Custom House★★

A couple of hundred metres along the Liffey bank, due east of the ever busy O'Connell Bridge, stands the **Custom House★★**, a Dublin landmark for over two centuries. With its long riverside façade and classical tower and 38m- (125ft) high dome, it is one of the city's architectural showpieces. It was designed by James Gandon (co-designer of the Four Courts) and completed in 1791. It was gutted in 1921 during the War of Independence and has subsequently been rebuilt. Today it is used by local government. An exhibition on two floors details the building's history, examines some of Dublin's social issues, and also gives a glimpse of the Custom House's original grand interiors (open daily, summer; Wed-Fri and Sun, winter).

Parnell Square

This is the oldest of the city squares after St Stephen's Green, laid out in 1748 as home to the cream of Georgian Dublin society. On the south side is the **Rotunda Hospital**, founded in 1748 as Europe's first purpose-built maternity hospital. It is famous for its exuberant Rococo **Chapel★** which is open by appointment only.

The north side of the interior of Parnell Square is taken up by the **Garden of Remembrance**, dedicated to all those who have died in the cause of Irish freedom. Also on the north side is the square's most splendid buildings, Charlemont House, which now holds the **Hugh Lane Municipal Gallery of Modern Art★** (closed Mon). Visitors are greeted by a large floor display of modern and contemporary artworks of all

The impressive Custom House reflected in the River Liffey.

kinds, which reflects the original Modern Art Gallery objective of its founder, Hugh Lane. Although its acquisition of contemporary works continues, the main theme of the gallery is late 19C and 20C works by Irish and continental artists (some first-class temporary exhibitions are also staged). Near the entrance, don't miss the brilliant exhibits in the tiny Stained Glass Room. The highlight is *Eve of St Agnes*, by Harry Clarke, famous for his work on the Grafton Street branch of Bewley's Café.

The continental collection includes a handful of paintings by Manet, Monet and Degas, alongside other Impressionist works by artists such as Daubigny, Courbet and Corot. Several works by Jack B Yeats are featured, and at the very back of the gallery

The Hugh Lane Gallery provides an elegant setting for these modern works of art.

look out for the wide-ranging talents of Irish artist Roderic O'Conor (1860-1940).

The gallery's most important recent acquisition is the studio of Francis Bacon, donated in 1998, though its contents (including drawings, canvases, books and photos) will not be on permanent display until 2001. An unfinished self-portrait of Bacon, still on the easel when he died in 1992, is currently on display.

Do be aware if you are coming to view specific works that there is a sharing arrangement on some of the most important pieces with several other major international galleries. Music lovers should visit on a Sunday to hear the 'Sundays at Noon' free concert series, which have been going strong since 1976 (held on around 30 Sundays a year; ☎ 874 1903 to check dates).

Just a few doors away are two more fine Georgian houses, now home to the **Dublin Writers' Museum**. This focuses on the lives and works of Dublin's many literary celebrities. It's a formal, fairly mundane sort of exhibition, with a case or two devoted to the books, letters, portraits and personal items of each of Dublin's better known literati, from world-famous writers such as James Joyce to less familiar names like Lady Gregory or John Synge (who wrote *Playboy of the Western World*).

A headphones tour summarises the salient points of each author's life and career, and provides an excellent starting point for a literary tour of Dublin. Upstairs is a magnificently decorated gallery, with a superb **stucco ceiling***, painted doors, an ornamental colonnade and gilded frieze.

For more in a similar vein, fans of James Joyce need only walk a block or two east to

Dublin Writers' Museum not only contains interesting exhibits, but is worth visitng for the elegant rooms, such as this saloon.

the **James Joyce Centre** in North Great George's Street. Also set in a beautifully restored Georgian mansion, this is less a museum than a study centre. Tours are given (on request) by Ken Monaghan, the extremely personable and very knowledgeable nephew of Joyce. It's nirvana if you're already a devotee but, perhaps surprisingly, it's also a good place to get started. Don't miss the excellent video of turn-of-the-century Dublin.

Just off Parnell Square to the north-west is the **National Wax Museum**. It may sound like a good bet for a rainy afternoon if you have children, but the overall standard is not of a high quality. Take them to the nearby IMAX cinema instead (*see* p.106).

National Botanic Gardens★★

Established in 1795, the **National Botanic Gardens★★** occupy a charming peaceful area of some 20ha (50 acres) beside the Tolka River. They feature a bog garden, a rose garden, a peat garden and an arboretum, providing almost all-year-round colour, but the star attractions are the three beautifully restored curvilinear glasshouses, built 1843-69 by Richard Turner, responsible for the Palm House at London's Kew Gardens. The riverside walk leads to the peat and bog gardens surrounding the ornamental lake, and on to the arboretum.

Next to the gardens soars a 51m- (167ft) high landmark – the Round Tower, a modern replica of the type of medieval tower found at monastic sites such as Glendalough. It lies in the grounds of the **Glasnevin Cemetery** and marks the grave of Daniel O'Connell. Other Irish heroes buried here include Michael Collins, Charles Stewart Parnell, Eamon de Valera and Brendan Behan. Cemetery tours are given (free of charge) every Wed and Fri at 2.30pm (meet at the main gate).

Escape from the bustle of the city in the leafy National Botanic Gardens.

City of Ink

The Irish literary tradition is one of the most illustrious in the world and it is remarkable that such a small country has produced so many world famous writers. Sadly, however, many of its most talented sons – including Oscar Wilde, Bram Stoker and George Bernard Shaw – left the country at an early age and seldom returned or even wrote about their native land. Others, such as Samuel Beckett and James Joyce, also went into voluntary exile but retained their affection for Dublin and reflected it in their works.

Samuel Beckett (1906-89) An enigma. His master work, *Waiting for Godot,* is still waiting for an explanation while *Breathe* (literally two men inhaling) is the shortest-ever stage play on record, lasting just a few seconds. Small wonder that he was a leading figure in the Theatre of the Absurd.

Brendan Behan (1923-64) Ever ready for a beer and a brawl, Behan has spawned almost as many anecdotes and one-liners as Oscar Wilde. A rabid Republican, he spent much time in jail, most famously for shooting at a policeman – though they say he was too drunk to hit him. He went on to write *The Hostage, The Quare Fellow* (quare meaning unusual) and *Borstal Boy,* before drinking himself into an early grave.

Portrait of Jonathan Swift, by Charles Jervas (1675-1739).

James Joyce (1882-1941) put Dublin on the map in 1922 with his extraordinary masterpiece, *Ulysses,* which detailed scores of city locations. Joyce famously claimed that should Dublin be destroyed it could be rebuilt from the pages of his book, though this should be taken metaphorically rather than literally. It was loved and hated for its groundbreaking, obscure and bizarre style and often controversial content. Although widely regarded as a classic of the 20C, it remains a difficult read (*see* p.92).

Jonathan Swift (1667-1745) was not only a great writer but dean of St Patrick's Cathedral for 32 years. Although *Gulliver's Travels* has become a children's classic, it was in fact a thinly veiled attack on 18C Anglo-Irish society. Even more biting was his *Modest Proposal*, a satirical pamphlet advocating that Ireland could rid itself of poverty and overcrowding in one go by selling its children for high-class English dinner table consumption – though not everyone saw the humorous side of it!

You can learn much about the city's literary heritage at The Dublin Writers' Museum but a much more lively introduction is the Jameson's Literary Pub Crawl tour (*see* p.104).

Follow the progress of Leopold Bloom, the fictional hero in James Joyce's novel Ulysses, *on his travels around Dublin. Fourteen of these bronze plaques in the pavement chart part of the route taken by Bloom on 16 June 1904.*

WEST OF THE CITY CENTRE

Most of the following attractions are within walking distance of the city centre. Kilmainham is a brisk 30-minute trot or you can take the 51 or 79 bus (from Aston Quay) to the Gaol and the Royal Hospital. The National Museum at Collins Barracks and Phoenix Park are both a short distance from Kilmainham on the north bank of the Liffey.

South of the River

Guinness Hopstore★

Tucked away in a wing of the giant brewery whose beery aroma frequently permeates the whole of central Dublin, the **Guinness Hopstore★** is a museum-style exhibition which tells you almost everything you wanted to know about Ireland's most famous drink. Do note, however, that this is not a working brewery tour and you are not admitted to any part of the actual production process.

A Guinness advertising icon of yesteryear.

For most visitors, the area dealing with Guinness advertising is the most fascinating. The first floor deals with the brewing and packaging of Guinness, and the cooperage gallery has a fascinating video illustrating the dying craft of barrel-making. However, there are no prizes for guessing that the most popular part of the exhibition is the bar, a large jovial place where each visitor gets to sample a pint (or bottle) of the Black Stuff.

If you are walking to the brewery (10 minutes from Christchurch Cathedral), an entertaining diversion is the oldest market in Ireland, Mother Redcap's Market (*see* p.108) and pub (*see* p.101), tucked away just off the main High Street.

Kilmainham Gaol Museum★★

No matter what the weather is outside, the cold stone cells and the terrible injustices of Kilmainham Gaol will chill you to the bone. Essential history.

Spending two to three hours in a grim, forbidding gaol may not be top of most visitors' lists, but it's a rare person who comes away from Kilmainham Gaol unmoved or, at the very least, possessing a far greater appreciation of the trials and tribulations of the emerging Irish nation. It's a cold place in every sense, so wrap up warmly (closed Sat in winter).

The gaol was built in 1796 as a general house of punishment and correction. However, it soon became inextricably linked with political prisoners, the place where the leaders of almost every major rebellion against British rule from 1798 up to 1916 were detained and often executed. Over 140 prisoners were hanged or shot here, including Patrick Pearse and the other leaders of the 1916 Easter Rising.

Before your guided tour of the prison, spend time in the excellent modern museum section. This is the best place in Dublin for getting the background and facts of the country's many uprisings. Here too you can study the hangman's techniques, and learn that during the Great Famine a 13-year-old boy caught stealing turnips would be sent to Kilmainham Gaol for two weeks (being in possession of a stolen loaf meant one month). Although in many ways

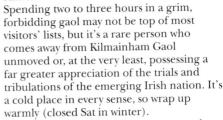

progressive for its day, the regime was still mind-numbing in others, with a typical example of 'correction' consisting of prisoners moving heavy cannonballs from point A to point B, then back to A again.

The guided tour of the prison is at once lively, informative, depressing and moving. It includes the crumbling cells where many famous prisoners were confined, the chapel where Joseph Plunkett was poignantly allowed to marry Grace Gifford immediately prior to his execution, and the great central gallery, familiar to anyone who has seen *In the Name of the Father*, which was filmed here.

After 128 years and over 100 000 detainees, the gaol finally closed in 1924. It had become a national institution and a symbol of Irish martyrdom. The very last prisoner released, fittingly, was Eamon de Valera, who went on to become prime minister and president of Ireland.

Kilmainham Gaol Museum, the most notorious of Ireland's prisons, is a grim reminder of Irish martyrdom.

Royal Hospital Kilmainham**, Irish Museum of Modern Art

The **Royal Hospital Kilmainham** was built between 1680 and 1684 as a home for retired and invalided soldiers. It was inspired by Les Invalides, in Paris, and pre-dated London's famous Royal Army Hospital in Chelsea by two years.

The complex comprises four ranges of buildings around a central courtyard, and once held up to 300 old soldiers. The last of these left the hospital in 1927 and it fell derelict until restoration in the 1980s. Today, the hospital is regarded as the finest 17C building in Ireland.

Since 1990 it has been home to the **Irish Museum of Modern Art** (IMMA), and three sides have been modernised and converted to galleries. In the North Range, however, the Great Hall and the chapel, famous for its unique Baroque stucco ceiling, survive and are open for tours on Sundays, 2.30pm and 3.30pm.

Once the home of retired soldiers, the Royal Hospital Kilmainham now houses the Irish Museum of Modern Art.

North of the River

Phoenix Park★★

The largest enclosed urban park in Europe, Phoenix Park covers a huge area of over 709ha (1 752 acres), twice as big as Hampstead Heath, over two-thirds the size of the Bois de Boulogne. Its name is a corruption of the Gaelic *fionn uisce*, pronounced *finn isch-ke*, meaning clear water. The land was confiscated from Kilmainham Priory in 1662 by the Duke of Ormond, who introduced a herd of fallow deer whose descendants still roam the area known as the Fifteen Acres (which actually covers some 300 acres!).

Most points of interest are just off Chesterfield Avenue, long and straight, which bisects the park, though it's quite a long walk between them. The park runs a shuttle bus service in summer, otherwise you will need your own transport.

Almost immediately to the right of the entrance is the **People's Garden**, the only part of the park to be formally planted, comprising a charming area of lawns, a small lake and flower beds. Opposite, to the left, is the landmark 61m- (200ft) tall **Wellington Memorial**, commemorating the Duke of Wellington, who was born in Dublin in 1769.

A little further into the park is **Dublin Zoo★**. It dates back to 1830 and is the second oldest in Europe. However, it has recently been refurbished to a

The Wellington Memorial in Phoenix Park is said to be the highest obelisk in Europe.

high standard and many of its animals are now displayed in a cage-free environment, separated from the public by ditches and/or large glass panels. The Zoo has a good variety of animals, including all the usual crowd-pleasers, and for the millennium an ambitious 13ha (32 acre) African Plains project will provide a new, naturalistic home for giraffes, hippos and rhinos.

Further along, past the polo grounds on the right, is the official residence of the President of Ireland (Aras an Uachtaráin), built 1751-54. Queen Victoria stayed here in 1849, and a young Winston Churchill also spent three years at the adjacent Little Lodge while his father and grandfather were based here. Opposite, a small road leads to the **Papal Cross**, a 27m- (80ft) high stainless steel monument to the visit of John Paul II, who in 1979 celebrated mass in the park with a congregation estimated at nearly one million people.

The **Park Visitor Centre**, housed in an old stable block, relates the history of Phoenix Park. Its most infamous incident occurred in 1882 when the Invincibles, a Republican splinter group, murdered the Vice-Regal Chief Secretary and Undersecretary in the park. A plaque in the road by the polo grounds marks the spot. Adjacent is a 17C tower house known as **Ashtown Castle**, while the building on the other side of the avenue is the United States Embassy.

National Museum of Ireland (Collins Barracks)★★

The dull, grey, two-dimensional façade of the Collins Barracks belies the superb National Museum decorative arts collection that relocated here in 1998 (closed Mon).

The building, named after Michael Collins, dates from 1701 and, until it was decommissioned in 1997, claimed to be the world's oldest continually occupied barracks.

The collection is both national and international, eclectic and wide-ranging in its tastes. Displays are of a very high quality. There's no better place to start than **The Curator's Choice**, 25 objects that have been chosen by the curators as a subjective introduction to the museum. Items change periodically, but are likely to include a Burne-Jones tapestry, an Irish hurdy-gurdy (musical instrument), Japanese bells, astronomers' astrolabes, methers (ancient Irish drinking vessels) and Louis Comfort Tiffany glass.

In a similar Aladdin's Cave fashion is the **Out of Storage** collection, featuring a cabinet of curiosities displayed in a modern warehouse style, as if the items really are still in storage. Totally unconnected, a sumptuously decorated 18C palanquin (a covered litter or Oriental sedan chair) sits close to a life-belt and oars recovered from the *Lusitania*.

The tour continues in a more traditional vein with gleaming displays of Irish **silver** and some beautiful **ceramics**, including the famous Fonthill Vase (1300-1325), one of the earliest documented pieces of Chinese porcelain to reach Europe.

The **Museum at Work** is a hands-on area showing the mechanics of restoration and research, focusing on specific case studies. You can, for instance, hear what the Cloyne Harp, made in 1621, and just restored, sounds like. Period furniture, scientific instruments and Irish country furniture fill the museum's other main exhibition areas.

The National Museum of Ireland – a museum which dares to assume subjective choices and takes the trouble to justify them.

Restored after being shelled in 1921 during the Civil War, the majestic Four Courts building looks out over the Liffey at Inns Quay.

The Four Courts

Like the General Post Office building, the Four Courts is a handsome neo-Classical Dublin landmark which has become famous more for a momentous event in the history of the emerging Republic than for its own intrinsic value. The year was 1921 and the episode was, like that of the General Post Office, a siege. Anti-Peace Treaty Republicans had occupied the building and, as a siege of two months had failed to dislodge them, the Free State forces finally shelled the rebels into submission.

The building was designed in 1785 and housed then, as it does now, the main law courts. Gutted in 1922, it has been superbly restored. The courts are open to the public when they are in session, but on any weekday between 11am and 4pm it is worth stepping into the vestibule under the great landmark dome to partake in the general hubbub, and witness lawyers and their clients milling to and fro.

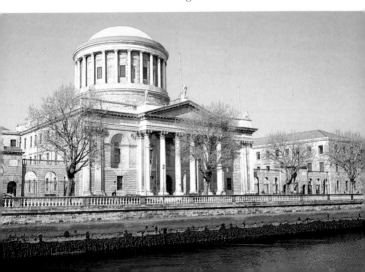

The magnificent organ in St Michan's Church, with the beautifully carved panel depicting musical instruments below.

St Michan's Church

St Michan's Church is the city's most unusual visitor attraction, renowned for its 'mummies' in the vaults beneath. In fact, they are not mummies at all but corpses which have been remarkably preserved by the very dry air, constant temperatures and methane gas below the church. The most recent body dates from the mid 19C and the oldest is thought to be a Crusader, some 700 years old. Most of the coffins, too, are in a fine state of repair, with their original velvet and brass studs still quite apparent. As a bonus, the tour guide is one of Dublin's finest, revelling in his unique circumstances!

The church itself is most famous for its 16C organ, on which it is said Handel played *The Messiah* in 1742. In front of the organ gallery, don't miss the unknown apprentice's masterpiece carving of 17 instruments, crafted from a single block of wood.

Old Jameson Distillery

Jameson's Bow Street distillery is the company's original home and dates from

1780. Production stopped here in 1972, though the company headquarters remain on the site. The Old Jameson Distillery, where visitors are educated into whiskey lore, is in fact a former warehouse where the old distillery has been re-created.

The tour begins with a slick audio-visual presentation extolling the virtues of *Uisce Beatha* (pronounced *ish-ke bah-ha*, meaning Water of Life), as Irish whiskey was originally known. Then it's on to see the old mash tun, the wooden fermentation vessels, the gleaming bulbous copper pot, the bottling lines and various other equipment which once helped turn out Jameson's finest. After the tour, five lucky individuals are chosen to be tasters, comparing Irish to Scotch and Bourbon, and standard Jameson's to superior older brands. Everyone, however, gets to sample a drop of Jameson's (*see* p.97 for more on Irish whiskey).

Antique copper stills at the Old Jameson Distillery, where fine whiskey was produced for years.

IN AND AROUND DUBLIN BAY

Stretching from Howth in the north to Dalkey in the south, Dublin Bay is a scenic stretch with several visitor attractions and is, quite literally, a breath of fresh air compared to the crowded city. Thanks to the Dublin Area Rapid Transport light railway (DART), exploring the bay area couldn't be easier. Jump on at any one of Dublin's three mainline railway stations and it's less than 30 minutes to either end of the DART line. Along the route, look out for the characteristic Martello Towers, gun emplacements built 1804-06 to counter the threat of a Napoleonic invasion.

Howth★ (north)

Howth★ (it rhymes with *both*) is a steep rounded peninsula of rock rising to form the northernmost jaw of Dublin Bay. It is renowned for its **cliff walks** and there is a footpath all around the peninsula: north past the Nose of Howth and Balscadden Bay is the most scenic route, while that to the south past the Bailey Lighthouse has fine

A fishing boat returns to the harbour, Howth.

views★ over Dublin Bay.

The village of Howth has been a **fishing port** for centuries, and its colourful fleet still makes an important contribution to the local economy. Adjacent to the fishing harbour is Howth's new symbol of wealth, its modern **yachting marina**. For a fine view over the marina, climb the adjacent Martello tower mound. Beyond is the small islet known as **Ireland's Eye**, where the early Christians built a 6C church, now in ruins; today the island is a bird sanctuary, visited by local boats in summer. Looking landward from the mound you can peer into the roofless semi-ruin of **St Mary's Abbey**, which dates from the 13C.

A little further inland is **Howth Castle**. This 16C pile is not open to the public, but the rhododendron **gardens** (beyond the Golf Club House) are worth a visit, particularly in late spring. The estate also includes the **National Transport Museum**, a modest collection despite its name, set in a barn beside the castle (open daily June-Aug; rest of year weekends only, noon-5pm).

Malahide (north)

Just north of Howth, Malahide is not served by the DART but is still easily reached by suburban rail, connecting with the DART at Howth Junction. Like Howth it is a colourful, attractive little seaside town, even if its brand-new marina development looks out of place.

The main attraction is **Malahide Castle★★**, a 20-minute walk from the centre through the leafy Malahide Demesne (pronounced *domain*, meaning estate). The oldest part of the castle is its 14C tower, where the splendid **Oak Room** is said to be the finest

early panelled room in Ireland. There's also a classic 15C **Great Hall**, though all the other rooms are 18C apartments. The estate also holds a beautiful 8ha- (20 acre) **botanic gardens** (open summer only) and the **Fry Model Railway Museum**. The largest of its kind in Ireland, the intricate handmade models faithfully reproduce the area and its railway system, including the DART railway. It will delight children and impress adults.

Malahide Castle was home to the Talbot family for 791 years.

Marino Casino** (north)

In the northern suburbs of Dublin, the Casino at Marino (casino in this context simply means small house) was designed in 1765 in a classic Palladian Greek-cross style by Sir William Chambers as a pavilion for the grounds of the now-defunct Marino House. Its squat single-room, single-storey appearance is a clever piece of *trompe l'oeil* design, as it actually holds 18 small rooms on two storeys and features elaborate plaster ceilings and inlaid wooden floors (open April and November, Thur and Sun, afternoons only; May-October, daily).

The marina, Dún Laoghaire.

Dún Laoghaire (south)

Dún Laoghaire (pronounced *dun leary*) is the main seaport entry from Britain, and ferries constantly chug in and out of port. Its most distinctive feature is its two long concrete piers, which when built (1817-42) formed the world's largest man-made harbour. The **East Pier**, which includes a bandstand, is the more attractive and in summer becomes quite animated. Walking the length of it (2.6km / 1.6 miles) to the red-and-white painted lighthouse is a traditional local pastime. For a little more excitement, sign on for the **Dublin Bay Sea Thrill**, where you are dressed like a lifeboatman, then propelled along in an inflatable at seriously high speeds (summer only). Still on the nautical theme, the former Mariners' Church on Haigh Terrace is home to the **National Maritime Museum**. Alongside a huge lamp from Howth's Bailey Lighthouse and a French longboat captured during Wolfe Tone's failed invasion of 1796 are historical curiosities, models and exhibits.

Marino Casino – an example of architectural ingenuity.

Sandycove (south)

Half a mile (0.8km) due south of Dún Laoghaire along the coast road, and quite visible from the East Pier, is Sandycove, a pretty little unspoiled bay with its own DART station. James Joyce stayed in the Martello tower here for six days in 1904 as the guest of the poet Oliver St John Gogarty, and the first chapter of *Ulysses* is set in the tower. Today it is home to the **James Joyce Museum** (open Apr-Oct), featuring first editions, letters, photos and personal effects. It's worth a visit just for its setting and there's a good **view** from the gun platform on the roof. Just behind is the locally famous Forty Foot beach where hardy bathers take a dip, traditionally naked, all year round.

Dalkey (south)

A few minutes' drive further south on the coast road and you come to the pretty little seaside village of Dalkey (pronounced *dol-key*) – Dublin Bay's most prestigious

Looking across Sandycove Bay to the James Joyce Tower.

Killiney Bay, with Bray Head and the Wicklow Mountains in the background, seen from Dalkey.

Shooting through the railway tunnel and emerging into picture-postcard Killiney Bay – no wonder Dublin's millionaires choose to live here!

address, popular with high-flying commuters who live here and well-heeled city visitors who come at the weekend to sample Dalkey's fine eating establishments.

The small High Street features two fortified buildings almost opposite each other: **Goat Castle**, now home to a Visitors Centre, and **Archbold's Castle**. But the real beauty of Dalkey lies in its setting. Take a walk out along Coliemore Road, past Dalkey Island, onto the coastal Vico Road. Just past Sorrento Point, marked by a colourful terrace of highly desirable properties, a magnificent **view**★★ of Killiney Bay, often compared to the Bay of Naples, opens out. Keen walkers should head up the steps, over the top of Dalkey Hill to **Killiney Hill Park**, with its wonderful views south to Bray Head and the Wicklow Mountains. Alternatively, you can simply stay on the DART and as the train rushes out from the tunnel just beyond Dalkey station the view of the bay is superb.

EXCURSIONS FROM DUBLIN

The Wicklow Mountains★★

The **Wicklow Mountains★★**, which provide the rolling backcloth to south Dublin, is a beautiful area of high peaks and spectacular views, lakes, reservoirs and waterfalls, open moorland and verdant valleys. Its most famous, though not its tallest, feature is the **Great Sugar Loaf Mountain**, rising to 502m (1 654ft).

Any coach excursion to Glendalough will show you a reasonable chunk of the Wicklow Mountains, though if you want to travel independently the St Kevin's bus, which takes a very scenic route, is recommended (ask for a timetable at the tourism office). This is a regular scheduled service and it's a nice slice of everyday Irish life to hear the driver greeting passengers by name and having some banter with them. There are also dedicated Wicklow Mountain coach tours, though to explore this area in detail you may wish to hire a car. For those with

Great Sugar Loaf Mountain.

time to spare and plenty of energy, the **Wicklow Way** is a long-distance footpath which runs north-south along the mountain range. The air will refresh and invigorate and the views and scenery are sure to soothe away cares and worries.

Glendalough★★★

Glendalough★★★ (pronounced *Glenda-loch*) is not only one of the most important historical sites in Ireland, it's also one of the most beautiful and atmospheric, with buildings and ruins set amid glorious countryside and the majestic backdrop of the Wicklow Mountains.

The Round Tower at Glendalough is a reminder of the site's religious, though not always peaceful, history.

Founded in the 6C by St Kevin, the monastery of Glendalough became one of the most pre-eminent religious centres in Europe and attracted students and pilgrims for many centuries. It was plundered intermittently by Vikings and Irish raiders and was finally destroyed by English forces in 1398.

Start your tour at the excellent Visitor Centre. A few yards away is the main **monastic site★★★**. Clustered around the ruined **cathedral★★** is a graveyard of old Celtic crosses, leaning at drunken angles, the oldest of which is St Kevin's Cross, unmissable at 3.7m (12ft) tall. Towering above all at 33m (100ft) is Glendalough's signature landmark, the **Round Tower★★**.

It was built in the 10C or 11C as a belltower to summon the monks to prayer, and also provided refuge from attack.

By the compact little 11C **Church of St Kevin★★**, follow the marked footpath, right, to Glendalough's two lovely lakes. Just before you get to the **Upper Lake★★** turn uphill, just off the main path, to the atmospheric ruined **Reefert Church★**, traditional resting place of kings and perhaps even St Kevin himself. Nearby is Kevin's Bed, a tiny cave used by the saint during his time of solitude at the monastery.

Glendalough's Upper Lake, in the heart of the tranquil Wicklow Mountains.

Powerscourt★★

The glory of **Powerscourt★★** lies in its **gardens**, a supreme mix of man-made and natural landscapes at the heart of one of Ireland's most scenic estates.

The gardens are laid out on a steep south slope facing the majestic Sugar Loaf Mountain, so that the visitor descends into an arcadian idyll, totally surrounded by mature trees and shrubs. The scale and grandeur of the project may be measured by the magnificent **Italian Garden terraces**, which alone took 100 men 12 years to complete. These descend to the focal **Triton Lake** and its 30m- (100ft) high fountain. To the left, the lake is flanked by an exquisite **Japanese Garden** and the Tower Valley with its **Pepperpot Tower** and North American trees. To the other side is the pleasingly

Great Sugar Loaf Mountain provides a scenic backdrop for the lovely Italian terraces and formal gardens at Powerscourt.

eccentric Pets' Cemetery (including the grave of Eugenie, the Jersey cow, who produced 17 calves and over 100 000 gallons of milk), the Dolphin Pond and the Walled Garden, with the longest herbaceous border in Ireland. Don't miss the gardens' three ornate wrought iron gates, the finest of which date from 1770 and came from Bamberg Cathedral, in Bavaria.

Some 5km (3 miles) from the house is the famous Powerscourt **Waterfall★★**, formed by the Dargle river which plunges 122m (400ft) in a thick white curtain down a jagged grey rock face. It's a wonderful area for a picnic and walking, and deer are a common sight.

Powerscourt House in its present form dates from 1730, though there has been a castle here since around 1300. The house possessed some of the finest 18C interiors in all Ireland, until gutted by a devastating fire in 1974. In 1996 the huge task of restoration began. This will not be complete for many years, but it is possible to wander through several bare rooms, some stripped back to their 16C stonework, and there is an excellent exhibition on the history of Powerscourt.

Stone statue of a dog, Powerscourt estate.

The ground floor of the house is now home to a number of high-class shops selling Avoca woollens, children's toys and clothes, souvenirs, Irish comestibles, music and more. Finally, don't miss the café. The quality of food is outstanding, and on a sunny day lunch on the terrace overlooking the gardens is pure heaven (but do get there early to get a seat).

There are plenty of guided coach tours to Powerscourt, but this is not a place to be rushed. Take the picturesque DART bayside route south to Bray, and then catch the Alpine Coaches minibus. This excellent service shuttles between the charming village of Enniskerry (2km from Powerscourt), the house and gardens, and the waterfall. In summer buses run frequently, at other times ☎ 286 2547 for details, or ask at Dublin tourism office.

Russborough House★★★

This superb Palladian mansion shares the same designer as Powerscourt (Richard

Castle) and was built in 1741-51. Also like Powerscourt, it enjoys the Wicklow Mountains' backdrop and an ornamental lake. However, Russborough is visited very much for its house (as opposed to its gardens), which is famous on two accounts: its richly decorated stucco interiors and, more importantly, the **Beit Art Collection**.

The art collection was built up in the late 19C by Alfred Beit, a co-founder of the De Beers diamond company. His nephew, Sir Alfred Beit, acquired Russborough in 1952 and inherited the collection which includes many European Old Master paintings, outstanding bronzes, porcelain, silver, furniture, tapestries and carpets (open Apr, Oct, Sunday only; May, Sept, Mon-Sat, 10.30am-2.30pm, Sun, 10.30am-5.30pm; June-August, daily, 10.30am-5.30pm).

The magnificent Russborough House, near Blessington, houses a fine art collection.

Newgrange★★★

Some 50km (30 miles) north of Dublin is the fertile valley of the Boyne, inextricably linked with Ireland's past, from prehistoric times through to the famous Battle of the Boyne in 1690. **Newgrange★★★** is the centrepiece of the Brú na Bóinne ('dwelling place of the River Boyne') complex of prehistoric passage tombs, recognised as one of the world's most important archaeological landscapes. Older than the Pyramids and Stonehenge, Newgrange dates back over 5 000 years, and so far is the only Brú na Bóinne tomb to be excavated. A visitor centre at the entrance to the complex tells what is known of the early Celts who built these tombs, before a mini-bus takes you to the actual tomb where a guide will accompany you inside.

A 19m- (62ft) long, claustrophobically

narrow stone passage leads to the small cross-shaped tomb chamber. Above, the tomb is covered by an inordinately large grassy mound the size of a football pitch. The tour is illuminating in every sense, with the highlight being a re-creation of the entry of sunlight into the chamber. The rays stream in through a small window-like opening over the door, creep up the passage and eventually enter right into the heart of the tomb. This phenomenon occurs naturally on just five days a year, on and around the winter equinox, and lasts for approximately 17 minutes (clouds permitting), but is simulated for visitors each day.

   Note: it is strongly recommended that you travel to Newgrange with a tour operator (e.g. Gray Line), as travelling independently by public transport is expensive and slow.

Newgrange is one of the best examples of a passage grave in Europe.

Moreover, Newgrange also gives priority to pre-booked coach parties. Individual pre-booking is not possible, so visitors risk arriving to find 'full up' signs.

Castletown House★★

Standing on the River Liffey, **Castletown House★★** was the first great Palladian mansion to be built in Ireland (1722) and is still remarkable today for its size and ornate decoration.

The original restrained 18C scheme of interior decoration, which used only local wood and stone, is preserved in the Brown Study. By contrast are the Red Drawing Room and the Green Room, with their rich damask and silk wall coverings and gilded decorations. The Print Room is a rare 18C survivor of the bygone ladies' custom of cutting out favourite prints and sticking them directly onto the walls.

The tour continues through several more apartments with its highlight being the final room, the Long Gallery, whose vivid blue, red and green decor in the Pompeiian style dates from the 1770s. Look through its windows to see two curious structures. The Conolly Folly, also known as the Obelisk, mounted on two tiers of arches, was built in memory of William Conolly. The Wonderful Barn is a conical structure comprising four diminishing brick domes with an external spiral staircase, used for drying and storing grain. Both were erected philanthropically by the house owner, Katherine Conolly, to create employment during the severe winters between 1739 and 1743 (note there is no public approach or access to either structure). The house is open Apr-Oct, daily (closed Sun am).

ENJOYING YOUR VISIT

THE SPIRIT OF DUBLIN

It's often said that visitors flock to Dublin not to see its sights but to experience the atmosphere of the city. And there is no better place, both metaphorically and literally, to imbibe the spirit of the place than in one of Dublin's pubs, or bars, as they are more often called here. After all, as the locals might say, who needs an Eiffel Tower or British Museum when you can happily spend the afternoon in a comfy pub drinking the world's best Guinness, chatting away, singing along to live music and perhaps watching the latest young Riverdancers hammering the boards.

One of the reasons why Dublin is such a great pub city, more so than London, is because of their numbers and proximity to one another. Compared to most major European cities, Dublin is a mere village and it has more than its share of village 'locals' – around 900 at the last count. It's no wonder then that people like James Joyce and Brendan Behan drank in so many places. The sheer availability and welcome of Dublin pubs makes them hard to pass by.

Of course, many bars have succumbed to the passing years and 'progress', and have been either demolished or turned into hideous 'tourist pubs'. Thankfully, however, these are the exception and there are still a remarkable number of good traditional pubs left in the city.

Yet Dublin isn't just a city for imbibing alcohol, far from it; the café society now so popularly imported into the UK from continental Europe has been thriving in Dublin for over a century, albeit on a smaller scale. Coffee in Bewley's is an unmissable part of the local scene.

The literary spirit of Dublin is also very much alive, not in the inanimate exhibition cases of the Writers' Museum, but in the brilliant wit and repartee of the Jameson's Literary Pub Crawl guides. For a gentler, almost dreamy pairing of literature and refreshments visit the Winding Stair Café; even better, turn on and tune in to one of their poetry readings.

For all its rich heritage, Dublin is not a city stuck in the aspic of its Celtic myths, its Georgian past or its Joycean heritage; feel the pulse of the new turn-of-the-century city, with the yuppies at Café-en Seine, the terminally trendy at the Clarence Hotel or the new Bohemians of Temple Bar.

To get a feel of Dublin before you leave home, hire out *The Commitments*, set and shot in the suburb of Kilbarrack, for its gritty Irish humour (and wonderful soul music) and *Michael Collins* for its many famous Dublin street and building locations and a more-or-less accurate version of the events following the 1916 Easter Rising. If you're the hardy literary type try reading Joyce's *Ulysses* – but don't worry if you don't understand all, or even much of it! For more contemporary reading pick up anything by Roddy Doyle, author of *The Commitments*.

Watching the world go by on the Grand Canal.

WEATHER

The Romans called Ireland *Hibernia*, meaning 'the land of perpetual winter', but the east coast is the drier side and, as exotic plants in many a garden attest, Dublin, warmed by the Gulf Stream, has a relatively mild climate for its cool northern latitude. The sunniest months are often May and June, the warmest (and among the wettest) are July and August, when the average maximum temperature is 19-20°C. At any time of year be prepared for rain and, as temperatures can fluctuate unpredictably, it is a good idea to dress in layers which you can add to or take off, as the weather dictates.

ENJOYING YOUR VISIT

CALENDAR OF EVENTS

March: *Dublin Film Festival* Irish and foreign films are screened throughout the city and its suburban multiplexes (very popular so book in advance).

17 March: *St Patrick's Day* ('Paddy's Day') is the biggest city event of the year with a parade of floats, marching bands and entertainers, and a wonderful fireworks finale. Traditional music festivals are held for a week around the 17th. Visitors from New York or Chicago, however, may be disappointed as to the scale of festivities compared to those at home.

Around March-April: *Six-Nations Rugby Internationals* Any rugby international featuring Ireland playing at home (at Lands-downe Road, just outside the city centre) turns the city into a raucous but good-natured rugby festival for the weekend.

Around 16 June: *Bloomsday Festival* Bloomsday, 16 June 1904, was the day on which Joyce chronicled Dublin in his groundbreaking novel *Ulysees*. Nowadays, the Bloomsday Festival covers a whole week. The name comes from Leopold Bloom, one of the two central characters of the book. There are various events at the most notable Joycean locations, both real and fictional, ranging from Sandycove by Dún Laoghaire to Glasnevin cemetery, and of course all over the city centre, where most of the story took place. Afficionados dress in Edwardian period costume. The festival is organised by the James Joyce Centre.

Third weekend July: *Temple Bar Blues Festival* This is the city's biggest musical celebration, featuring Irish, UK and US artists often of considerable stature. Past names include B B King, Buddy Guy and Taj Mahal.

September: *All Ireland Hurling Final* Witness this great Gaelic sport final in Croke Park (or on TV if you can't get tickets).

October: *Dublin Theatre Festival* A varied programme of new local talent, Irish and international companies (booking essential).

An event in the Bloomsday Festival.

ACCOMMODATION

Dublin has recently undergone a hotel-building boom so in theory there is no shortage of places to stay, particularly at the top end of the market. In practice, the city is often over-subscribed so you should book well ahead at all times. Many city centre **hotels** are expensive. A good alternative is a 3- or 4-star **guesthouse** or **bed & breakfast** (also called town houses) which can be as good as, if not better than, a middling 2- or 3-star hotel.

The cheapest option is **hostels**. There is only one official International Youth Hostel (61 Mountjoy Street, Dublin 7 ☎ 830 7766) but there are several other hostels providing cheap dormitory accommodation which are affiliated to Independent Holiday Hostels (IHH). If you are visiting during the summer months (June-end Sept), you can rent student rooms in Trinity College for a reasonable rate (£25 single to £75 for a flat or triple room for up to 3 people) ☎ 608 1177 fax 671 1267.

Dublin Tourism offices provide a booking service (for a small fee and a deposit). You can access information and make bookings using their internet address (http://www. visitdublin.com) or you can call Ireland Reservations free of charge, ☎ (international code+) **800 668 668 66** for credit card bookings.

The following prices are a guide to what you can expect to pay for a double room in a central hotel per night per person, usually with breakfast (but do check first). However, special off-peak rates and deals can dramatically reduce these prices.

5-star hotel: over IR£ 120
4-star hotel: IR£ 80-120
3-star hotel: IR£ 60-80
2-star hotel: IR£ 30-50

The Michelin *Red Guide to Great Britain and Ireland* lists accommodation and restaurants in Dublin and the surrounding area.

Recommendations

Expensive

The Merrion *Upper Merrion Street, Dublin 2* ☎ **603 0600** fax 603 0700 Dublin's newest 5-star hotel and part of the Leading Hotels of the World group, occupying four beautifully restored Georgian town houses (£210-260).
The Shelbourne *27 St Stephen's Green, Dublin 2* ☎ **676 6471** fax 661 6006 Dublin's Grand Old Dame is still probably the finest location in town, elegant

and refined without being stuffy or overbearing (£240-275).

Fitzwilliam *St Stephen's Green, Dublin 2* ☎ 478 7000 fax 478 7878 Perfectly located, this newcomer to the Dublin scene is set to become a modern classic, with understated luxury and award-winning restaurant (£210-260).

Clarence *6-8 Wellington Quay, Dublin 2* ☎ 670 9000 fax 670 7800 In the throbbing heart of Temple Bar and transformed by Bono and his U2 buddies into the coolest spot in town, the Clarence is the place to spot music and film stars. Individual stylish decor, every mod-con, great food (£180-200).

Moderate

Stakis Dublin *Charlemont Place, Dublin 2* ☎ 402 9988 fax 402 9966 Good value, modern and comfortable, within walking distance of the city centre. The rooms at the back are very quiet. Wonderful breakfast in an airy, modern restaurant looking onto the Grand Canal (£145-185).

Inexpensive

Jury's Christchurch Inn *Christchurch Place, Dublin 8* ☎ 454 0000 fax 454 0012 Never mind the modern carbuncle appearance, enjoy the central location, the comfortable rooms, and the flat-room rate (maximum 3 adults or two adults and 2 children) which makes a family stay very good value (£62).

Ormond Quay Hotel *7-11 Upper Ormond Quay, Dublin 7* ☎ 872 1811 fax 872 1362 Situated on

Elegance and style at the Shelbourne Hotel.

the banks of the Liffey, opposite the Temple Bar area (£70-150).

Outside Dublin

The Old Rectory *Wicklow* ☎ **404 67048** fax 404 69181 Victorian guesthouse situated just north of Wicklow on the R750. Good meals (dinner only); 7 rooms (£52-104).

Tinakilly House *Rathnew* ☎ **404 69274** fax 404 67806 Part Victorian country house hotel and restaurant 2km north-west of Wicklow. Extensive gardens, tennis court, 38 nicely furnished rooms, some with four poster beds (£117-144).

FOOD AND DRINK

The traditional food of Ireland is similar to that of much of Britain, based on potatoes and vegetables accompanying simple fish dishes and hearty meat dishes such as stews and pies. But, also as in much of Britain, food, and in particular eating out, has come on in leaps and bounds within the last few years. Whereas 'steak and chips' was once as posh as it got, it is a sign of the Dublin times to see posted on a pub menu 'fillet of beef with champ, smoked bacon and balsamic jus, accompanied by polenta biscuits with red capsicum salsa and basil pistou', even if this is a far from typical pub offering.

Breakfast

The full Irish breakfast should be sampled at least once during your stay, and typically comprises egg, bacon, sausage, white pudding, black pudding, potato cakes, tomatoes and toast. Fill up on this, and you'll only need a snack at lunchtime.

Traditional dishes

Ireland's national vegetable is the humble **potato**. The Irish consume on average 317lbs (144 kilos) per person per year. However, they are also a carnivorous nation and the most famous dish of all is the ubiquitous **Irish stew**. At its best, this is an unmissable casserole of hearty chunks of lamb in a mouthwatering gravy, with a generous root vegetable flotsam. Beware though, it can also be a disappointingly thin soupy affair with mutton instead of lamb. Traditionally, Irish stew is served with a scone, though it will generally also come with potatoes. Ireland's other national stew is **coddle**, a mix of layered pork, sausages, bacon, potatoes and onion.

When it comes to chops and steaks, lamb and beef are the favourite meats and the green fields and hills of Wicklow are famous for their lamb.

A **boxty** is a potato pancake cooked on a griddle, with

Pulling a pint of Guinness.

such as turbot and monkfish. Fresh from the Republic's clean, fast-flowing rivers, salmon is a popular dish.

Oysters and prawns are also taken locally, though these days the famously large Dublin Bay prawns (sometimes referred to as langoustines) are mostly exported and generally only appear on more expensive restaurant menus.

various stuffings or mixtures. The simplest is cabbage, similar to the English bubble 'n' squeak. Boxty occasionally turns up on the breakfast table, but the only place in town which makes a feature of them is Gallagher's Boxty House (*see* p.99).

Two other national potato dishes are **champ** – mashed buttery potatoes with peas and cabbage, parsley, chives and spring onions, and **colcannon** – a Harvest or Halloween dish of mashed potatoes, onions, parsnips and white cabbage, all mixed with butter and cream.

Fish and seafood

The Irish are proud of their piscatorial offerings and their fishing grounds produce sole, plaice, cod, haddock and hake, as well as more expensive items

Drinks

The drink of Dublin is **Guinness**. In almost every bar in the city you'll see 'the wine of Ireland' (as Joyce called it) knocked back in pints by hefty labourers and petite office secretaries alike. For the uninitiated few, the Black Stuff is a porter-style of beer which derives its distinct flavour from the malt and barley being roasted (giving it its dark colour) and its high hop content. It is much more bitter than most English beers and has a remarkably smooth and creamy body. Guinness is not Ireland's only porter; Murphy's is another example which is also brewed in the city, but Guinness is incomparably the most popular. One thing that almost everyone agrees upon is that Guinness is a notoriously bad traveller and that it tastes far better in Dublin than

Irish whiskey barrels.

fuel. Try it for yourself at the Jameson's Irish Whiskey Centre (*see* p.73).

Should you get caught out by one of Dublin's notoriously unpredictable showers, warm up with an **Irish Coffee**. This delicious national creation comprises a good measure of Irish whiskey, brown sugar and hot black coffee, topped with a layer of cream poured into the glass over the back of a spoon to keep it floating on the top, so it resembles a small Guinness. Sipping the hot coffee through the cold cream is sheer heaven – just beware of burning your lips!

Recommendations

As befits its latter-day cosmopolitan status, Dublin offers cuisine from most corners of the world. The biggest challenge is to find an Irish restaurant; there are very few of these and the best option for finding genuine Irish food is to try a pub. These can be the most congenial and cheapest places to eat, though beware – quality varies greatly.

Eating out in Dublin can be relatively expensive, but at lunchtimes and during the early evening (around 5pm-7.30pm), 'happy hour' prices in many establishments are drastically reduced. Here is a

anywhere else; logically, therefore, the very best pint is at the Guinness Hopstore (*see* p.64). Guinness is always drunk well chilled and is allowed a few minutes' settling time, so be prepared to wait at the bar – most Irish bartenders are very good at their job and your order will not have been forgotten!

It isn't just the spelling (note the extra 'e') that differentiates **Irish whiskey** from Scottish whisky ('Scotch'). There are two main taste differences: Irish whiskey is distilled three times compared to its cousin's twice, so it is smoother. Also, Irish whiskey does not have the characteristic smokey taste of Scotch. This is because Scotch barley is dried over smokey peat fires, whereas the Irish process uses anthracite, a smokeless

Bewley's Oriental Café, Grafton St.

selection of cafés, restaurants and pubs which capture the spirit of eating and drinking in Dublin. A meal in one of these places is cheap to moderately priced, except where indicated. Telephone numbers are given only where reservations are accepted.

Cafés
Bewley's Oriental Cafés
Whether you want a coffee and cake or a full meal, Bewley's is the quintessential Dublin café. The main branch, Grafton Street, is by far the most attractive of the three city centre

Bewley's, and the Harry Clarke Room should not be missed (reservations taken for the Harry Clarke Room only ☎ 635 5470). For a taste of Bewley's as it used to be, however, visit the little-changed branch at 12 Westmoreland Street (by O'Connell Bridge). This cavernous place has a marvellous earthy, slightly down-at-heel atmosphere, with its original red, plush, church pew-like settles, open fires with sturdy Victorian wooden surrounds, Chinese wallpaper and oriental screens. The food is good-value self-service buffet style. Sunday breakfast here is a local tradition. The original Bewley's

Café, founded in 1840, is at 13 South Great George's Street. It is similar in appearance, but smaller than the Westmoreland Street branch and not quite so atmospheric.

Winding Stair Bookshop & Café *40 Lower Ormond Quay*
A wonderful place for biblio-philes and anyone in search of good wholemeal salads, quiches and homemade cakes, all with a great view of the Ha'penny Bridge, if you're lucky enough to get a window seat (open Mon-Sat, 10.30am-6pm).

Café-en-Seine *40 Dawson Street* ☎ **677 4369** Dubbed Dublin's catwalk café, this was the first and is still one of the trendiest of the city's new wave Euro-style café-brasserie-bars. Its ultra-long bar, high ceiling and Parisian fin-de-siècle look draw yuppies by the score.

Fish and chips

Like the English, the Irish set great store by their 'chippers'.

Beshoffs *14 Westmoreland Street* Don't be put off by the American fast-food style service tills. Beshoff's has been a city institution since the turn-of-the-century and serves high quality excellent value fish and chips in Edwardian surroundings. Other city branches, notably at 7 Upper O'Connell Street.

Leo Burdock's *Werburgh Street, near Christ Church Cathedral* Leo Burdock's is famed throughout the city as the best 'chipper' in town. Take-away only (go to the small gardens opposite the cathedral).

Restaurants

Fitzers at the National Gallery *Merrion Square* ☎ **661 4496** Award-winning café-restaurant serving Mediterranean, European and seafood dishes at lunchtime (open gallery hours, until 8.30pm Thur). Even more fashionable branches at *Temple Bar Square* (☎ **679 0440**) and *51 Dawson Street* (☎ **677 1155**), both open until 11.30pm (expensive).

Cooke's Café *14 South William Street* ☎ **679 0536** Very stylish modern Mediterranean, Cali-fornian and seafood cooking (expensive).

Chapter One *18-19 Parnell Square* ☎ **873 2266** Elegant Georgian basement restaurant specialising in Modern Irish cuisine, particularly seafood and game (expensive; closed Sat lunch, Mon dinner, Sun).

Gallagher's Boxty House *20 Temple Bar* ☎ **677 2762** Boxties are the house speciality at this likeable informal restau-rant, but there are lots of other traditional Irish dishes, includ-ing their famous brown bread ice cream.

Kilkenny Design Centre
6 Nassau Street Traditional Irish food, carvery lunches as well as high-quality homemade soups, sandwiches and snacks (open Mon-Sat 9am-9pm, Thur 8pm).

The Tea Room *The Clarence Hotel, 6-8 Wellington Quay, Temple Bar* ☎ **670 7766** Not a tea room at all, but a hyper-trendy restaurant serving a splendid fusion of world cooking with Irish influences (expensive; closed Sat, Sun lunch).

Pubs
The Brazen Head *20 Lower Bridge Street* Slightly away from the central hubbub, this low dark ale house claims to be the oldest in all Ireland, trading for over 800 years. There are a number of rooms, including one ancient bar that must be the darkest in Dublin. By contrast is the charming small courtyard. Award-winning restaurant serving traditional Irish and continental cuisine (☎ **677 9549**).

Davey Byrne's *21 Duke Street* Probably the most famous of Dublin's many Joyce-related pubs, Davey Byrne's has changed over the years but is still a very pleasant bar, with some nice art-deco touches (*see* p.104). Restaurant serving traditional Irish and seafood cuisine (☎ **677 5217**).

Johnnie Fox's (Fox's Pub)
Glencullen, County Dublin (south of the city, very well signposted) Truly, madly, deeply 'Oirish' since 1798, Fox's is the sort of place you thought only existed in Irish films and the imagination, filled with every stereotypical Irish fitting and fixture you can think of. However, this is no theme pub, but the real thing, with traditional music every night. Award-winning restaurant specialising in fish and seafood (☎ **295 5647**).

Long Hall *52 South Great George's Street* Long and narrow, this very beautiful pub is over 200 years old but Victorian in appearance, with fine chandeliers and Art Nouveau glass panels.

McDaid's *3 Harry Street, off Grafton Street* Another strong claimant to be central Dublin's finest small pub; very Gothic and church-like, with its high ceiling and stained glass windows. It was once the city morgue and is famed as the drinking trough that finished off Brendan Behan.

Messrs Maguire *1-2 Burgh Quay* This fine example of a recently converted 'new-old' Dublin pub occupies four floors of a 19C premises overlooking the Liffey. It features some unusual little rooms, a library bar, a gourmet restaurant and its own brewery

– do sample its superb Ruby Porter.

Mulligan's *8 Poolbeg Street* A famous old-fashioned no-nonsense boozer ideally situated for passing travellers between the Hawkins Street bus terminus and Tara Street station. Local Dubliners appreciate the legendary Guinness served here.

Mother Redcap's *Back Lane, off High Street* Frequented by Mother Redcap market stall-holders and not a few local characters, this is a perfect place to while away a Sunday lunchtime, listening to the musicians.

The Norseman *29 East Sussex Street* Often cited by locals as the best pub left in the centre of Temple Bar, The Norseman is an attractive traditional drinking den. You might find room here when the others are bursting. Traditional music and jazz every night except Monday.

Oliver St John Gogarty *58-9 Temple Bar* Famous touristy pub in the heart of Temple Bar and the starting point of the Musical Pub Crawl (7.30pm daily, except Sat); usually jam packed, but worth a visit for its live music and upstairs restaurant serving good traditional Irish food (☎ **671 1822**).

The Brazen Head, reputedly the oldest pub in Ireland.

O'Neill's *2 Suffolk Street* Conveniently sited opposite the main tourist office, O'Neill's is a Victorian warren of rooms and bars. You'll probably find one, if not more, to your liking (*see* p.113).

The Palace *21 Fleet Street* Small but perfectly formed, The Palace is an unspoiled Victorian gem, snug and inviting. There's a back room and upstairs lounge, too – if you can get in.

Porterhouse *16 Parliament Street, Temple Bar* Dublin's first microbrewery and a labyrinthine new pub of several attractive rooms and bar spaces. Very trendy, terribly crowded and noisy – you'll either love it or hate it.

Stag's Head *1 Dame Court, off Dame Street* Together with the Long Hall, one of the most beautiful pubs in Dublin, ecclesiastical in character with a long mahogany bar, stained glass and ornamental metalwork. Good pub food.

Temple Bar *48 Temple Bar* Horribly packed at peak times, but otherwise a very pleasant traditional little place which puts on a packed programme of music, all using only 'passive amplification'.

Toner's *139 Lower Baggot Street* Over 200 years old and little changed for half that time, Toner's is a perfect example of an unspoiled, small Dublin pub.

Almost immediately opposite is **Doheny & Nesbitt**, very much in the same mould.

The Long Stone *College Green, Townsend Street* (near Tara railway station) A large pub on several levels with crazy decor, which resembles a grotto, an enchanted forest, a medieval castle and a press room! Friendly and lively atmosphere. Food served at lunchtimes and until 7pm.

ENTERTAINMENT AND NIGHTLIFE

Music

Dublin's best-known nightlife is listening to traditional music played in an informal setting in a pub. This is not entertainment staged just for tourists. Dubliners love it too. Several pubs offer music nightly, starting at around 9pm. The tourist office has a list of pubs which regularly host live traditional music, but if in doubt head for Temple Bar, which is the nightime capital of Dublin for just about most visitors' nocturnal activities. If you don't catch an evening session, many pubs also have live music on Sunday lunchtimes.

Taking traditional entertainment a stage further is the *hooley*, best translated as a party. The biggest and probably best staged hooley nights, or Irish cabarets, are nightly at **Johnnie Fox's** pub (*see* p.100) and at two hotel venues: **Jury's Hotel**, at Ballsbridge (just outside the centre), and **Doyle's Cabaret**, at the Burlington Hotel, on Upper Leeson Street, (both May-October only). In addition to music these offer traditional food, dancing and a comedian. A themed cabaret is offered by **Dublin's Viking Centre** (*see* p.45).

For a more contemporary Irish music feel, head for Wexford Street where a few doors from each other are two of Dublin's best venues for up-and-coming and established Irish bands, the **Mean Fiddler** and **Whelan's** (the latter is also a fine pub).

Other good venues where you can catch international name acts and high quality Irish bands are: **Vicar Street**, on the corner of Thomas Street West and Vicar Street; **HQ at the American Music Hall of Fame** on Middle Abbey Street; **Temple Bar Music Centre**, Curved Street, Temple Bar; **Eamon Doran's**, 3A Crown Alley, Temple Bar; and the **Harcourt** at 66 Harcourt Street. Look in the *Event Guide*, an indispensable free paper distributed in bars and cafés around town, or buy a copy of

Dublin's own music magazine, *Hot Press*, to find what's on.

A favourite night spot which guarantees a good time, no matter who is playing, is the venerable, atmospheric **Olympia Theatre** (72 Dame Street ☎ 677 7744).

If you're looking for visiting international superstars, check out who's playing **The Point** (East Link Bridge ☎ 836 3633), which caters for around 5 000 spectators at a time. It's about 20 minutes' walk from the city centre, but special buses run for some shows (tickets can be expensive). At the opposite end of the scale the **International Bar**, 23 Wicklow Street, is a nice intimate space to spot up-and-coming musical talent.

Comedy

As you might expect, Dublin has a thriving comedy scene.

ENJOYING YOUR VISIT

Places to experience the *craic* are **Murphy's Laughter Lounge**, (Thur-Sat) on Eden Quay, the **International Bar**, 23 Wicklow Street (Mon, Wed, Thur), the **Norseman**, East Sussex Street (Thur) and the **Ha'penny Bridge Inn**, Wellington Quay (Thur).

One of the most entertaining and funniest Dublin nights out is the **Jameson Literary Pub Crawl**. It starts at the Duke's pub, in Duke Street, where you will be treated to a short sketch from a famous Irish play and told a story or two about such Dublin literary legends as Behan and Joyce and their con-

Waiting for Godot *performed just a few feet away from you in a smoky Dublin pub, Guinness in hand – enigmatic, hilarious, quintessential Dublin!*

nection with the place in which you are drinking. The tour moves on to three or four more pubs and locations, where the exercise is repeated and a drop or two of the Black Stuff is consumed. The tour guides are professional actors who first and foremost entertain, but also impart a good wedge of the city's literary heritage. They are masters of the ancient Irish art of storytelling, and at times are downright hilarious. Don't worry about being ignorant of Irish literary history before you start – no previous knowledge is required to enjoy the tour. Tours go daily in summer; for winter times ask at the pub or in the tourism office (for bookings ☎ 670 5602).

Nightclubs

The Dublin club scene may be relatively small but is currently one of the hottest in Europe.

The famous Joycean Davey Byrne's pub, on Duke Street.

Buy a copy of the city's trendiest magazine, *In Dublin*, to see what's generally hip, and the *Event Guide* to see what's on. The *EH2* supplement from the *Evening Herald* may also help you.

Places that are very much in vogue include: **The Kitchen**, part of the super-cool U2-owned Clarence Hotel; the **PoD** (Place of Dance), Harcourt Street, but beware the tight door policy; and **Lillie's Bordello**, at Adam Court, off Grafton Street, haunt of super-models, rock stars and wannabes.

For something a little more interesting than techno, trance or the latest in Euro-thump music, get along to the **Gaiety Theatre** (South King Street ☎ 677 1717), where from 11.30pm each Friday and Saturday night you can enjoy live bands, dance to jazz, samba and salsa (they'll teach you how) or see a cult movie in the main theatre.

Older punters in search of a good old-fashioned mainstream disco might enjoy **Break for the Border**, on Lower Stephen's Street.

Performing Arts

The great Irish tradition of hard-hitting drama is maintained by **The Gate** (Cavendish Row, Parnell Square ☎ 874 4045) and **The Abbey** (26 Lower Abbey Street ☎ 878 7222), who put on classics and experimental works. Dublin's two other best known theatres are **The Olympia** (72 Dame Street ☎ 677 7744) and the **Gaiety Theatre** (South King Street ☎ 677 1717). Both produce mainstream and West End shows, as well as variety acts. Both also enjoy a split personality, becoming late night music venues.

The main city venue for classical music is the **National Concert Hall** (Earlsfort Terrace ☎ 475 1572). Two notable free concert venues are the **Bank of Ireland Arts Centre** (Foster Place ☎ 874 1903; Thur 1.15-2pm), and the **Hugh Lane Municipal Gallery** (Charlemont House, Parnell Square ☎ 874 1903; most Sundays at noon).

Dublin has no great tradition of, nor indeed regular mainstream venues for dance, ballet and opera, but nonetheless you can generally find something worthwhile in town. Consult the *Event Guide*.

Cinema

The city has plenty of cinema options; see the *Evening Herald* for details. The **Irish Film Centre**, 6 Eustace Street, Temple Bar, shows arthouse films, while at the other extreme is the **Sheridan IMAX 3D** cinema at the Parnell Centre, Parnell Street. Cinephiles will enjoy the acclaimed **Dublin Film Festival** each March.

CHILDREN

With its emphasis on pubs, history and literature, Dublin is very much a city for adults. If you do have children with you, however, the following places are worth knowing about.

The Ark, Eustace Street, Temple Bar, is an arts and cultural centre designed for local children (aged 4-14) but open to visitors too (note that most activities require pre-booking). Pop in and see what's going on. With its various buskers and street entertainment, Temple Bar in general is a lively place for kids.

The **gardens** and playgrounds of St Stephen's Green and Merrion Square are great for letting off steam (and feeding the ducks in the former). More formal attractions are: **Dublin's Viking Adventure**; the **Zoo**; the **Natural History Museum**; the **IMAX 3-D cinema** (all described in more detail in the *Exploring Dublin* section). The charming family-run **Lambert Puppet Theatre**, Clifton Lane,

Monkstown, has a museum and plays to suit children and adults alike.

The ride north along **Dublin Bay** on the DART is a low-key adventure in itself, and older thrill-seekers may enjoy the **Dublin Bay Sea Thrill**, at Dún Laoghaire – a high-speed, rather expensive inflatable boat ride around Dublin Bay. If the sun is shining, go to **Bray** which has a good beach and the **Sea Life Centre** aquarium.

Also out of town, **Malahide Castle**, which is actually a fortified mansion, features the **Fry Model Railway Museum** and a reasonable adventure playground. Take a picnic.

For **eating out** fast-food style try: the **Chicago Pizza Pie Factory** on St Stephen's Green, for its Sunday lunchtime children's entertainment; **Eddie Rockets** 1950s-style American diners, which are all over the city and serve excellent burgers; or the famous **Bad Ass Café**, Crown Alley, Temple Bar, where Sinead O'Connor once served burgers and fries.

SHOPPING

Dublin has an excellent selection of shops, even if prices, on the more affluent south side of the river at least, are relatively high.

South of the river

Dublin's main shopping area centres around Grafton Street. **Grafton Street** itself, pedestrianised and often jam-packed, always colourful, features several upmarket British chain stores and department shops. Its jewel is **Brown Thomas**, Ireland's best and most exclusive department store.

Behind Grafton Street is the **Powerscourt Townhouse Centre**, a superbly converted Georgian complex which has some good arts, crafts and fashion shops geared towards visitors, as well as lots of refreshment options. At the top of the stairs, the Design Centre showcases clothing by leading Irish designers. Adjacent is **George's Street Market**, a small charming wrought-iron and glass arcade filled by cheap clothing stalls, second-hand record sellers, a fortune teller and a couple of tasty food stalls. Continue along South Great George's Street for much of the same atmosphere.

At the St Stephen's Green end of Grafton Street is **St Stephen's Green Shopping Centre**, a large modern mall

St Stephen's Green Shopping Centre.

whose award-winning exterior design somewhat flatters to deceive, but still has a good range of shops for locals and visitors. At the other end, opposite Trinity College railings, **Nassau Street** hosts a row of specialist high-class Irish heritage shops (woollens, name plaques, music, crystal, china etc.). Don't miss the **Kilkenny Design Centre**, which features the very best of mainstream contemporary Irish design, including excellent woollens and ceramics. Its café is recommended too. Next to Kilkenny, at 14 Nassau Street, the **Celtic Note** is a music shop specialising in Celtic and Irish music.

Just around the corner, along **Dawson Street**, are more high quality shops, notably Hodges Figgis and Waterstones, two of Dublin's best bookshops, and the exclusive **Royal Hibernian Way** mall.

Temple Bar is one of the city's most interesting and eclectic shopping areas, ranging from cheap second-hand clothing to high bohemian fashion, and from world antiques and bric-a-brac to state-of-the-art household goods. At the cutting-edge of Irish design is the **DESIGNyard**, East Essex Street, a glittering showcase for jewellery, glassware, ceramics, textiles and furnishings. On Saturday there's a small **food market** at Meeting House Square, with lots of tempting ethnic and wholefood goodies.

Immediately west of the city's two Anglican cathedrals, in the area known as the Liberties, is **Francis Street**, Dublin's antique centre, with several shops selling all sorts of bona fide aged pieces, from the type of Nubian statues seen outside the Shelbourne Hotel, to Victorian fireplaces. For more portable antiques and flea-market items, try the enjoyable down-to-earth **Mother Redcap's market** (Fri-Sun only, 10am-5.30pm) on Back Lane, just off High Street.

North of the river

The shops may not be so glitzy on this side of the Liffey, but the main shopping thoroughfares of **Mary Street** and **Henry Street**, both just off O'Connell Street, are still worth perusing. The updated **Arnott's** on Henry Street and the more traditional **Clery's** on O'Connell Street are the main department stores.

Try **Eason's** on Upper O'Connell Street for their comprehensive, reasonably priced range of books and magazines. Also on the north side, next to the Ha'penny Bridge, don't miss the wonderful **Winding Stair Bookshop and Café** for the most atmospheric shuffle through the bookshelves in Dublin.

The city's most colourful market takes place daily on **Moore Street**, off Henry Street, where garrulous vendors selling fruit and vegetables, flowers, fish and meat keep alive the entrepreneurial spirit of Molly Malone. And in case you were wondering about the women at the edge of the market shouting ''bacco, 'bacco' (i.e. 'tobacco'), they are, quite blatantly, selling black-market cigarettes!

Out of town

The weekend market at **Blackrock**, just a 10-minute journey south of Dublin on the DART light railway, is Dublin's best general market. Clothes, antiques, crafts, furniture and general bric-a-brac are on sale, often at bargain prices (Sat and Sun, 10am-5pm).

More of a trek is **Avoca Handweavers**, at Kilmacanogue, near Bray. It combines its own beautiful clothes with lots of other traditional and contemporary Irish craft items, and throws in a good restaurant to make the journey worthwhile. Special buses make the trip twice daily, departing from O'Connell Street at 11am and 2pm.

Souvenirs and gifts

You'll find good quality souvenirs such as Celtic jewellery, Guinness memorabilia and musical items such as penny whistles and bodhrans all over town at reasonable prices.

For more expensive, high-quality typically Irish gifts look out for **woollens**, particularly those from Avoca Handweavers, and **crystal glass**, most famously by Waterford, who have recently added contemporary designs to their traditional range.

SPORT

The Irish are a passionate sporting race, avidly following horseracing and three types of football: rugby, soccer and Gaelic football. All football and hurling matches take place from August to May, and horseracing takes place most weekends of the year; see the sports pages of the local paper for details.

Horseracing is hugely popular, with the nearest course being Leopardstown (☎ **289 3607**), a short bus ride away. Close, too, is Fairyhouse (☎ **825 6167**), famous for its 3-day Easter festival meeting, culminating in the Irish Grand National. The Curragh (☎ **045 441 205**), Ireland's principal flat-racing course, is some 50km

(30 miles) away.

Peculiar to Ireland are Gaelic football and hurling, both closely entwined with Ireland's Celtic heritage and covered in some detail at the GAA (Gaelic Athletic Association) Museum at the Croke Park stadium (☎ 836 3222), where both sports are played.

Gaelic football is an exciting, very athletic sport, somewhere between rugby and soccer, with players allowed to kick and punch (but not throw) the ball into, or over, a combined rugby/soccer goalpost. On the third Sunday in September,

Croke Park is home to the All Ireland Final, Ireland's largest spectator event – the Gaelic football equivalent of the English FA Cup Final.

The nearest equivalent to **hurling** is hockey, though here too there are significant differences in the rules, the technique and attitude – hurling is played in a fierce attacking spirit, and has been described as a 'no-holds barred' form of hockey!

Rugby has a long pedigree in Ireland, and international matches are played at Landsdowne Road in the Dublin

Horseracing, Leopardstown.

suburbs. You will be in no doubt as to when a rugby match is on, as Dubliners will talk of little else for at least that weekend.

Football (soccer) was at an all-time high following the Republic's international team qualifying for the latter stages of the 1990 and 1994 World Cup finals. In the last few years, however, they have done less well in both the European and the World Cup finals. The international team also plays at Landsdowne Road. There are two local premier division teams, but the passion for the domestic game is nothing like as strong as it is in England.

Far and away the most popular visitor sport is **golf**. There are several courses, catering for all levels, some extremely beautiful and within just half an hour of Dublin centre. Pick up a copy of the *Visitor's Guide to Golfing in and around Dublin* from the tourist office, or contact Dublin Corporatation (☎ **834 7208**) for details of Corporation courses open to visitors.

Visitors looking for other forms of recreation (particularly if they have children in their party), have several other options. The Leisureplex group operate a number of 24-hour **ten-pin bowling** allies in the city and its suburbs (Malahide Road, Coolock, Dublin 17 ☎ **848 5722**; Village Green Centre, Tallaght, Dublin 24 ☎ **459 9411**; Stillorgan, Co Dublin ☎ **288 1656**). **Ice skating** is available at Dublin Ice Rink (Dolphin's Barn, South Circular Rd ☎ **453 4153**; Silver Skate Ice Rink, North Circular Rd, Dublin 7 ☎ **830 4405**). Or you could try your hand at **inline skating** at Rollerdome (Ballinteer Rd, Dundrum, Dublin 16 ☎ **296 1199**).

Popular with children and grown-up children alike, and providing a thrilling wet-day option, are the indoor **karting** circuits: Kart City (Old Airport Rd ☎ **842 6322**); Kylemore Karting Centre (off Naas Rd, Dublin 10 ☎ **626 1444**); Phibsboro Karting Centre (Cross Guns Bridge, Dublin 7 ☎ **830 8777**).

A more relaxing option may be **swimming**, though Dublin's public pools, mostly located in the suburbs, are on the small side. Check with the tourist office for details of opening times.

THE BASICS

Before You Go

Visitors entering Ireland from any country other than the United Kingdom should have a full passport valid for the period of their stay. (Visitors from the United Kingdom do not need a passport or visa). No visa is required for USA, Canadian, Australian, New Zealand or EU nationals. Other nationalities should check before travelling. No vaccinations are necessary.

Getting There
By Air

Dublin airport is 12km (7.5 miles) north of the city and handles domestic and international flights. The national carrier is **Aer Lingus** (☎ **705 6705** for flight information; ☎ **844 4777** for reservations) who, alongside Delta (USA flights), provide most transatlantic flights. There are several airline options from Britain; the cheapest fares are usually provided by **Ryanair** ☎ **0541 569 569** in the UK; **677 4422** in Dublin.

By Ferry

Both **Stena Line** and **Irish Ferries** run passenger-and-vehicle ferry services from Holyhead (on Anglesey) in North Wales, to Dún

Laoghaire (pronounced *dun leary*) some 96km (60 miles) due west. The standard crossing takes around 3½ hours, but Stena High Speed Sea Service (HSS) makes the crossing in just 1hr 40 minutes to Dún Laoghaire or to Dublin Harbour, only 3km (2 miles) from the city centre. Both companies offer at least four sailings daily. For Stena Line ☎ **0990 707070** in the UK; ☎ **204 7777** in Dublin. For Irish Ferries ☎ **08705 171717** in the UK, ☎ **661 0511** in Dublin.

By Train

Connolly Station, in the heart of town, is the terminus for trains from Belfast and Sligo to the north, and Wexford and Rosslare to the south. Heuston Station, 4km (2.5 miles) from the centre, is the terminus for Cork, Killarney, Limerick, Waterford, Galway, Westport and Ballina.

Train services from the UK are scheduled to connect with the ferries. For details of Inter-City trains, contact **Irish Rail** (Iarnród Éireann), Connolly Station, Dublin 1 ☎ **836 333**.

Arriving

A special **Airlink** bus service runs between the airport and city centre, and takes around 30 minutes. Buy your ticket at the machine by the bus stop or pay on board. Ordinary scheduled services 41, 41A, 41B and 41C also run the same route (departing from Eden Quay), are much cheaper, and only a few minutes slower than Airlink.

Bus no 53 is timetabled to meet Dublin Harbour ferry arrivals, and goes to North Walk. For Dun Laoghaire arrivals, the DART takes only 20 minutes into town.

Taxis are available from both places, but are expensive (around £15 from Dún Laoghaire).

Dublin city tour bus passing O'Neill's bar.

A-Z

Accidents and Breakdowns

Contact the rental firm in the event of an accident or breakdown. It is obligatory to carry a red warning triangle or to have hazard warning lights to use if you break down. If you have an accident, exchange names, addresses and insurance details. In an emergency ☎ **999**. *See also* **Driving, Emergencies**

Accommodation *see p.93*

Airports *see* Getting There, p.112

Banks

Banks are open Mon-Fri 10am-4pm (Thur until 5pm). Exchange bureaux stay open longer hours, but give a less favourable rate of exchange. ATM cash-dispensing machines can be found all over the city centre.

Bicycles

There are several cycle hire shops in the centre of town.

Ask for details at the tourism office. Beware that traffic is heavy and fast in the city centre.

Dublin Bike Tours guide visitors around the quieter streets and lanes, daily from April-Oct, meeting at the front gate of Christchurch Cathedral (Mon-Fri, 9.45am and 1.45pm, with a special dawn ride on Saturdays, meeting at 5.45am ☎ **679 0899**).

Breakdowns *see* Accidents

Camping

The nearest official site to the city centre is Shankhill (☎ **282 0011**) 10 miles (16km) south, in a pretty location 3km (2 miles) from Bray. There is a direct bus service and the DART into town. Pitches (82 in total) are not bookable in advance and soon go in high season. Contact the tourism office for further details.

Car Hire

There are numerous car hire

agencies at the airport and port. Rates are among the highest in Europe, but local firms are usually significantly cheaper than international operators.

The lower age limit is generally 23 and in most cases you must have held a full licence for at least two years. Make sure that collision damage waiver is included in the insurance. Automatics should be reserved in advance and are more expensive.
See also **Driving, Accidents and Breakdowns**

Churches see **Religion**

Climate see **p.91**

Clothing

Pack warm clothes for winter, and even in summer you should bring a light jacket and jumper as nights can be cool. As the weather is unpredictable, it is best to dress in layers and at any time of year be prepared for rain, which may be sustained in winter and showery in spring and summer. If you are cold, there is no shortage of high-quality Irish woollens to keep you warm.

Casual wear is the norm, although you will look out of place at Dublin's smarter restaurants and hotel dining rooms unless you have made an effort.

Most clothing measurements are standard throughout Europe but differ from those in the UK and the USA. The following are examples:

Women's sizes

UK	8	10	12	14	16	18
Europe	38	40	42	44	46	48
US	6	8	10	12	14	16

Women's shoes

UK	4.5	5	5.5	6	6.5	7
Europe	38	38	39	39	40	41
US	6	6.5	7	7.5	8	8.5

Men's suits

UK/US	36	38	40	42	44	46
Europe	46	48	50	52	54	56

Men's shirts

UK/US	14	14.5	15	15.5	16	16.5	17
Europe	36	37	38	39/40	41	42	43

Men's shoes

UK	7	7.5	8.5	9.5	10.5	11
Europe	41	42	43	44	45	46
US	8	8.5	9.5	10.5	11.5	12

Consulates and Embassies

Australia
2nd Floor, Fitzwilton House, Wilton Terrace, Dublin 2
☎ 676 1517

Canada
65 St Stephen's Green, Dublin 2 ☎ 478 1988

New Zealand
46 Upper Mount Street,
Dublin 2
☎ 676 2464

UK
31 Merrion Road, Ballsbridge,
Dublin 4
☎ 205 3700

USA
42 Elgin Road, Ballsbridge,
Dublin 4
☎ 668 8777

Crime

The centre of Dublin is, by and large, a safe place for visitors, though after dark do stick to the main, well-lit streets. Petty theft is a problem, however, as indicated by the fact that almost every shop along the major thoroughfares has its own door security person. You should take the usual precautions, and beware of pickpockets in crowded places such as Grafton Street, and be careful where you put your bags in pubs, cafés and restaurants.

Note that Fitzwilliam and Merrion Squares and the neighbouring streets are prime prostitution areas, and should be avoided at night. Avoid walking in city parks after dark, especially Phoenix Park, and sit downstairs on buses.

If you have a car, try to park it in a secured garage or space and do not leave any valuables inside.

Currency *see* **Money**

Customs and Entry Regulations

There are no restrictions on goods brought into Ireland from EU countries, though limits apply to other countries.

For goods taken out of the country, the normal EU regulations apply to EU residents:
200 cigarettes *or* 100 cigarillos *or* 50 cigars *or* 250g tobacco
2 litres port, sherries, sparkling wine *or* 1 litre spirits
60ml perfumes
250ml toilet water

USA and Canadian citizens may take home up to $400 and $300 worth of goods respectively, as well as their tobacco allowances.

There are no restrictions on taking currency into Ireland, but you cannot take out more than IR£100.

Disabled Visitors

For guides to facilities and accommodation services in Dublin, contact in the UK: **RADAR**, 12 City Forum, 250 City Road, London EC1V 8AF ☎ **(0171) 250 3222**; the **Holiday Care Service**, 2 Old

Bank Chambers, Station Road, Horley, Surrey RH6 9HW ☎ **(01293) 774535**.

In Dublin, contact the **National Rehabilitation Board**, 44 North Great George's Street ☎ **874 7503**, which produces the useful booklets *Guide for Disabled Persons* and *Accommodation Guide for Disabled Persons*. **The Irish Wheelchair Association**, 24 Blackheath Drive ☎ **833 5366**, and the **Disability Federation of Ireland**, Sandyford Office Park, Dublin 18 ☎ **295 9344**, are other helpful organisations.

Driving

For visitors not used to the European style of relatively fast driving along narrow roads, driving in Dublin may well be intimidating. However, you certainly don't need a car to get around town and with the city centre congested at most times of day (dreadfully so at rush hours), a car is a liability rather than an asset.

Street parking is always difficult, and tow-away restrictions are strictly enforced, though you should be able to make parking provisions with your hotel.

Most excursions are well covered by public transport and coach excursions.

However, if you wish to explore the countryside, particularly in and around the Wicklow Mountains, then a car is the best method. Traffic outside Dublin is relatively light.

Remember that the rules of the road are basically the same as mainland Britain; drive on the LEFT and give way to traffic coming from the right.

Petrol stations are frequent in and around the city but don't venture into the countryside running on empty as you may travel miles before the next one. Petrol stations are open daily (many are closed Sunday mornings) and prices are comparable to the UK, i.e. much more expensive than in the USA. Carry cash for small provincial stations, which may not accept credit cards.

Main road surfaces are usually fine, but off the beaten track you may have to slow down for tractors, sheep, dogs and other rural hazards.

The following speed limits apply: 100kph/60mph on all out of town roads, 50-64kph/30-40mph in towns, as posted. Note that speed limit signs are posted in miles per hour.

Seat belts are compulsory and children under 12 must travel in the back of the car. *See also* **Accidents and Breakdowns**

Electric Current
The voltage in Ireland is 220/240V. Plugs and sockets are of the square-fitting three-pin variety.

Embassies see Consulates

Emergencies
For all emergency services ☎ 999. These calls are free.

Etiquette
The Irish are a very friendly, easy-going people and there is little in the way of formal etiquette that will trouble you.

Guidebooks see Maps

Health
The standard of health care in Ireland is first class. In theory, EU residents can take advantage of the reciprocal free medical treatment arrangement, provided that a completed E111 form is held. In practice, you may end up paying for it and then claiming a refund at home. Be sure to keep all receipts to support your claim.

Non-EU residents are charged for all non-emergency treatments and it is vital to have holiday insurance which covers this eventuality.

Hours see Opening Hours

Information see Tourist Information Offices

Language
Aside from a few pockets in the remote and rural western parts of the country where Irish/Gaelic is still the primary tongue (called the *Gaeltacht*), English is always the first language. However, there has been a recent resurgence in Gaelic and it is a compulsory school subject.

Many city centre signs are bilingual and occasionally are in Gaelic only; buses, for example, going to the city centre are signed *An Lar*.

To the uninitiated, Gaelic is a very difficult language, with pronunciation varying wildly from its English appearance, but don't worry – probably the only Irish word you need is the drinking toast *slainte*, roughly pronounced *slan-ge* (with a soft g sound), meaning '(to your) health'.

Lost Property
Report the loss of any valuable item to the police and keep a note of their reference number for any subsequent insurance claim.

Airport ☎ 704 4481
Dublin Bus ☎ 703 3055
Irish Rail ☎ 703 2587
Taxis ☎ 475 5888

Maps and Guidebooks

The *Michelin Red Guide Great Britain and Ireland* contains detailed information on hotels and restaurants throughout Ireland, including Dublin. The *Michelin Green Guide Ireland* has detailed information on the main sights and attractions in Dublin, detailed street maps of the city and information on other towns and attractions you may visit as excursions from Dublin. The **Road Map 923 Ireland** will help with route-planning. The most portable and undoubtedly the cleverest city centre map is the *Dublin Popout Map* by Compass (available from the National Gallery shop, and other places), which pops out from little bigger than credit card size to a 9½in by 10½in (24cm by 27cm) sturdy, clear and detailed map of the centre.

Money

The monetary unit is the Irish pound or punt, pronounced *poont*. It is written IR£ or simply £, but should not be confused with the UK £ sterling which is a separate (and higher value) currency. Like the UK £ it is divided into 100 pennies. Notes come in denominations of IR£5, IR£10, IR£20 and IR£50; coins come in 1p, 2p, 5p, 10p, 20p, 50p and IR£1.

Johnson's Gate, off Grafton Street.

All major credit cards are accepted in most city centre establishments. Hotels and many large shops will also accept travellers' cheques, though you may be charged at a lower rate of exchange.

There are no restrictions on the amount of currency that visitors can take into Ireland, but you may not leave with more than IR£100. Banks and exchange bureaux can be found at the airport, seaport and all over the city.

See also **Banks**

Newspapers

British and foreign newspapers and magazines can be bought, and are often on sale the same day. The *Irish Times* and the *Irish Independent* are the two main national dailies, while Dublin's *Evening Herald* (Mon-Sat) has a useful listings supplement. For events listings, consult *In Dublin* or the free *Event Guide*.

Opening Hours

Shops: Traditional shop hours are Mon-Sat 9/9.30am-5.30/6pm, with late opening (until 7.30/8pm) on Thursday. Temple Bar shops may not open until 10am or later. A good number of shops now also open on a Sunday afternoon.

Chemists: These open traditional shop hours, with a rota system ensuring at least one chemist per neighbourhood is open late in case of emergencies (its address is posted in the window of the other chemists and is also listed in the *Evening Herald*. O'Connell's, 55 O'Connell Street, is open until 10pm daily.

Museums: Normal opening hours are Mon-Sat around 10am-5/6pm, and Sun 2pm-5/6pm. Some close on Monday.

Pubs/bars: The official opening hours are Mon-Sat 10am-11.30pm in summer, until 11pm in winter and on Sunday 12.30-2pm and 4-11pm or 11.30pm all year (unless food is served, in which case all day opening is permitted). However, some pubs have a late drinking license for an extra hour or two, and during this time charge extra for drinks.

Police (the Garda)

Police officers (colloquially called the gards) wear a navy uniform. They are usually friendly and approachable. The main station is in Phoenix Park ☎ 677 1156. In emergency ☎ 999.

Post Offices

Post Offices are usually open

A jaunty statue of James Joyce outside Café Kylemore, on Earl Street North, just off O'Connell Street.

Mon-Fri 9am-5.30pm and Sat 9am-1pm. The main post office, the historic landmark on O'Connell Street, is open Mon-Sat 8am-8pm and Sun 10am-6.30pm. There is also a post office conveniently situated opposite the main tourism office on Suffolk Street.

Stamps may be bought at a limited number of newsagents

(a sign is usually posted in the window) as well as at post offices. It costs 32p to send a letter (up to 20g) to EU countries, 52p to USA, and postcards cost 28p (EU) or 38p (USA). Post boxes are painted green.

Poste restante mail should be addressed to the person, Poste Restante, GPO, O'Connell Street, Dublin 1.

Public Holidays

New Year's Day: 1 January
St Patrick's Day: 17 March
Good Friday: variable
Easter Monday: variable
May Day: First Monday in May
Whit Monday/June Holiday:
    First Monday in June
August Holiday: First Monday
    in August
All Soul's Day/October
    Holiday: last Monday in
    October
Christmas Day: 25 December
Boxing Day/St Stephen's Day:
    26 December

Religion

The Republic of Ireland is predominantly a Roman Catholic country and mass is celebrated every Sunday. However Dublin's two main cathedrals are Anglican and there are churches of most denominations in the city. Enquire at the tourism office for addresses and times of services.

Smoking

Smoking is banned in most public places.

Taxis *see* Transport

Telephones

Public telephones can be used to call anywhere in the world. They accept either coins or telephone cards, available from newsagents in denominations of IR£2-10.

Cheap rates apply 8pm-8am Mon-Fri and all over the weekend.

For operator ☎ 10
For international operator
☎ 114
For local directory enquiries
☎ 1190
For UK directory enquiries
☎ 1197
For international directory
enquiries ☎ 1198

Country codes are as follows:
Australia ☎ 00 61
Canada ☎ 00 1
New Zealand ☎ 00 64
UK ☎ 00 44
USA ☎ 00 1
To call Dublin from abroad,
☎ 00 353 1

Time Difference

The Republic of Ireland is on GMT (i.e. UK time). The clocks go forward one hour between late March and late October, making it the same as Central European Time. Ireland is 5 hours ahead of US Eastern Standard Winter Time.

Tipping

If a service charge is not included in the restaurant bill, and the service and food have been good, then leave a tip of around 10 per cent. It is also customary to tip the hotel-room maid 50p-£1 per day. A good tour guide deserves a tip of £1-2 (depending on the length of the tour), and a polite and helpful taxi driver should also be given a tip of around 10 per cent. Porters, doormen, bellhops and so on, should be given anywhere between 50p and £2, depending on the service performed.

It is not customary to tip bartenders in cash. If you want to show your appreciation, offer them a drink instead (don't be offended if they take the cash equivalent).

Tourist Information Offices

The **Dublin Tourism Office**, housed in a beautifully renovated old church building on Suffolk Street, is an excellent one-stop place to begin your tour of Dublin. Try to go first thing in the morning as it gets very busy.

If you want general information and/or accommodation, the first thing to do is to take a numbered ticket from the automatic dispenser, then watch the screens for your number to be shown. While you wait your turn to be attended to, you can browse in their very well stocked souvenir and gift shop, which also has an excellent range of books.

As well as seeking general information, you can book tours, theatre tickets, car hire, Irish Ferries tickets and change money. There's also a good café upstairs. The centre opening hours are: Sept-June, Mon-Sat 9am-5.30pm, closed Sun; July-Aug, Mon-Sat 9am-6pm, Sun 10.30am-2.30pm ☎ **1850 230 330** (recorded information only).

The e-mail address is: **reservations@dublintourism.ie** (for accommodation); **information@dublintourism.ie** (for general enquiries). The web site address is **www.visitdublin.com**

There are other offices at: **Dublin Airport**, Arrivals Hall (open daily July-Aug 8am-10.30pm; rest of year Mon-Sat 8am-10pm) **Dún Laoghaire** ferry terminal (open Mon-Sat 10am-6pm) **Exclusively Irish**, 14 Upper O'Connell Street (open Mon-

Sat 10am-1.30pm and 2-5.30pm)

All accept personal callers only.

Unrelated to the official tourist board, but still worth a visit for up-to-date news of what's on, is the **Temple Bar Information Centre**, 18 Eustace Street, ☎ 671 5717 (open Mon-Fri 9am-5.30pm, Sat-Sun 11am-4pm).

The **Irish Tourist Board** is known as **Bord Fáilte**. They have a walk-in Dublin office at Baggot Street Bridge, Baggot Street (open Mon-Fri 9.30am-12.30pm, 1pm-5pm), or you can write to them at PO Box 273, Dublin 8.

Bord Fáilte offices abroad:
Australia: 36 Carrington Street, Sydney, NSW 2000
☎ **(02) 929 96177**
UK: 150 New Bond Street, London W1Y 0AQ
☎ **(0171) 493 3201**
USA: 345 Park Avenue, New York, NY 10154
☎ **(212) 418 0800**

Tours

There are all sorts of walking tours and bus tours within and outside the city. For details of all of these, enquire at the main tourism office or see the free newspaper the *Event Guide*. The following tours are all mentioned in the body of this guide: **Jameson's Literary Pub Crawl** (*see* pp. 90 and 104); **Dublin Bike Tours** (*see* p.114); the **Musical Pub Crawl** (*see* p.101).

The best of the many history-themed tours is **Historical Walking Tours of Dublin**, who meet at the gates of Trinity College at noon (daily May-Sep; Sat-Sun only Oct-Apr).

Transport

Dublin is a compact city, and the quickest way to get about is often to walk. However, for

A familiar part of the Dublin skyline – an old whiskey distilling tower by the Guinness factory.

slightly longer distances you will want to use the bus, while the DART is an invaluable suburban service. Only consider a car for touring outside the city (*see* **Driving**).

Bus: The dedicated commentary-included **tour buses** are useful as a means of orientation and as an introduction to the city's sights, but are expensive to use just as a means of getting from A to B. So you'll have to use the ordinary scheduled bus service, run by **Dublin Bus**. These are often crowded, unpunctual and have the infuriating habit of arriving in pairs.

Many services demand the correct money and do not give change, so it's as well to keep a selection of coins on you. However, if you do have to overpay at least you get a Passenger Change Receipt which you can use to get your cash back at the Dublin Bus office, 59 O'Connell Street. You can enquire here also about pre-paid tickets (available daily, weekly or monthly which, if little else, save you the hassle of handling cash), a route map and timetables.

A **Nitelink** service operates on Thursday, Friday and Saturday, hourly from half past midnight to 3.30am, departing from the termini at College Street, D'Olier Street and Westmoreland Street, to all suburban areas. The bus number and destination is displayed on the front of each bus (in English and Gaelic), though to the consternation of many a tourist, city-bound buses only advertise their direction in Gaelic, *An Lar*, meaning 'city centre'.

DART: The Dublin Area Rapid Transport (DART) railway system services Dublin Bay and passes right through the city centre, stopping at all three railway stations. By contrast with the bus service, the DART is fast, punctual (every 5-10 mins at peak times, 15 mins off peak), clean, efficient, cheap and a model of how an urban light railway scheme should operate. They do, however, get very crowded in the city during rush hour.

Taxis: These can be prebooked, taken from a taxi rank or, if you're lucky, hailed in the street. All work on the meter. Beware at peak times – they can get caught in the traffic and end up being very expensive. Look in the local directory for a full list of numbers, but here is a selection:

Co-Op Taxis ☎ **676 6666**
Access Taxis ☎ **668 3333**
City Cabs ☎ **872 2688**
All Fives Taxis ☎ **455 5555**

TV and Radio

RTE is the national broadcast-ing company, offering two channels: RTE1 and Network 2. All British TV channels are generally available and most hotels of a reasonable standard also provide a wide choice of satellite and/or cable channels.

RTE is also the principal radio broadcasting station, with news and current affairs on RTE1, youth-oriented music on 2FM and classical music on FM3. There are any number of independent local stations on the FM band.

Vaccinations
see **Before You Go, p.112**

Water

The tap water is perfectly safe to drink.

INDEX

accommodation 93-95
Act of Union 13
Anna Livia Fountain 55

Bank of Ireland 30, 31
  The Story of Banking
  30
Battle of Kinsale 10
Battle of the Boyne 11,
  87
Beckett, Samuel 62
Behan, Brendan 62
Bewley's Oriental Cafés
  26, 31, 90, 98
Bray Head 79
Bray Sea Life Centre 106

Castletown House 89
Chester Beatty Library 45
children 106
Christ Church Cathedral
  46-47
  crypt 47
  Strongbow's
  monument 47
Collins, Michael 15, 19,
  43
Connolly, James 16, 17
County Wicklow 26
craic 21
Custom House 13, 56, 57

Dalkey 26, 78-79
  Archbold's Castle 79
  Goat Castle 79
DART railway 26, 74, 75,
  76, 78, 79, 86, 106
de Valera, Eamon 15, 16-
  17, 18, 66
Dublin Bay 6, 26, 74-79
Dublin Castle 42-45

Great Courtyard 43-44
Powder Tower Under-
  croft 44
Record Tower 43
State Apartments 44
Dublin Writers' Museum
  59, 60, 63, 90
Dublin's Viking
  Adventure 45-46, 106
Dublinia 47
Dún Laoghaire 77
  Dublin Bay Sea Thrill
  77, 106
  East Pier 77
  National Maritime
  Museum 77

Easter Rising 15, 16-17,
  55, 65, 91

famines 9, 14
festivals and events 92
Fitzwilliam Square 12
food and drink 95-102
Four Courts 13, 71

General Post Office
  Building 17, 55
Glasnevin Cemetery 61
Glendalough 8, 26, 82-83
  cathedral 82
  Church of St Kevin 83
  monastic site 82
  Reefert Church 83
  Round Tower 82
  Upper Lake 83
Government Buildings
  40-41
Grafton Street 31-32, 107
Grand Canal 91
Great Sugar Loaf
  Mountain 80
Guinness 96
Guinness Hopstore 64

Ha'penny Bridge (Liffey

Bridge) 5, 25, 53
Howth 26, 74-75
  Castle 75
  National Transport
  Museum 75
  St Mary's Abbey 75

IMAX cinema 60, 106
Irish Civil War 18, 19
Irish whiskey 73, 97

James Joyce 4, 36, 59, 62,
  63, 78, 91, 121
James Joyce Centre 60
James Joyce Museum 78
Jameson's Literary Pub
  Crawl 25, 63, 90, 104

Killiney Bay 79
Killiney Hill Park 79
Kilmainham Gaol 24, 65-
  66

Lambert Puppet Theatre
  106
Leinster House 40
Liffey Bridge see
  Ha'penny Bridge

MacNeill, Eoin 16
Malahide 26, 75-76
  Castle 75-76, 106
  Fry Model Railway
  Museum 76, 106
Marino Casino 76, 77
Marsh's Library 50, 51
Merrion Square 12, 24,
  41-42
Molly Malone statue 30,
  31
Mother Redcap's Market
  108
museums and galleries
  Dublin Civic Museum
  33
  Hugh Lane Municipal

INDEX

Gallery 57-59
Irish Museum of Modern Art (IMMA) 67
National Gallery 38-39
National Museum 24, 37-38
  Collins Barracks 24, 69-70
National Wax Museum 60
Natural History Museum 40, 106
State Heraldic Museum 38
music 21, 22-23, 102-103

National Botanic Gardens 61
National Library 38
Newgrange 87-89
Newman House 35-36
Number Twenty Nine 42

O'Connell Street 54-56
O'Connell, Daniel 14, 41, 54
Old Jameson Distillery 72-73

Parnell Square 12, 6-60
Parnell, Charles Stewart 56
Pearse, Patrick 16, 17, 65
Penal Laws 11
Phoenix Park 68-69
  Ashtown Castle 69
  Dublin Zoo 68-69, 106
  Papal Cross 69
  Park Visitor Centre 69
  People's Garden 68
  Wellington Memorial 68
Plunkett, Joseph 16, 17
Powerscourt 26, 84-85
  House 85

Italian Garden terraces 84
Japanese Garden 84
Pepperpot Tower 84
Triton Lake 84
Waterfall 85
Powerscourt Townhouse Centre 32-33, 107
Pro-Cathedral 56
pubs 90, 100-102

River Liffey 5, 6, 7, 71
Rotunda Hospital 13, 56-57
Royal Canal 6
Royal Hospital Kilmainham 67
Russborough House 86-87
  Beit Art Collection 87

Sandycove 78
Shelbourne Hotel 35, 93, 94
shopping 106-109
Sinn Fein 15
sport 109-111
St Michan's Church 72
St Patrick's Cathedral 48-49
  Boyle monument 49, 50
St Stephen's Church 42
St Stephen's Green 12, 33-36
  Fusilier's Arch 34
  Shopping Centre 107-108
Statute of Kilkenny 9
Swift, Jonathan 63

Temple Bar 20, 26, 51-53, 108
theatres 103-104, 105
Trinity College 24, 25, 230

Book of Kells 24, 28, 29
Library 24, 29
The Dublin Experience 29
Treasury 24, 29

University Church 36

War of Independence 18, 56
weather 91-92
Wicklow Mountains 6, 26, 79, 80
Wicklow Way 82
Wilde, Oscar 41, 62

Yeats, W B 41